TA
and
the manager

dudley bennett

a division of american management associations

Library of Congress Cataloging in Publication Data
Bennett, Dudley
    TA and the manager.
    Bibliography: p.
    Includes index.
    1. Psychology, Industrial.   2. Management.
    3. Transactional Analysis. I. Title
HF5548.8.B377   158.7   76-20559
ISBN 0-8144-5422-4
ISBN 0-8144-7511-6 pbk

First AMACOM paperback edition 1978.

preface

THIS BOOK arose out of action. The organization development movement originated in the early sixties. It has many fathers, not the least of whom were Richard Beckard, Herb Shepherd, and Leland Bradford. OD, now over 15 years old, has gone through a number of stages. Team building, survey feedback, job enrichment, and the organizational mirror are solid developments of those early years. However, by the mid-sixties it was clear that the productivity of these sociotechnical strategies was limited because we were unable to control for the variable of human behavior. Typically a manager would comment, "Your rational problem-solving sequence is great, but how do you get it off the wall and make it work with people?" In addition, when it became clear that distrust was corroding the group process, and when people held discussions about what kinds of behavior build trust, they did so in terms from which it was difficult to generalize.

Team building has always worked better than participants anticipated, yet important issues remained unexplored because individuals didn't have the skills to deal with them. Sometimes a participant would shut off discussion: "I don't think we should talk about that here. It'll just get people upset and off the track. No one here is trained to handle it." Few individuals wanted to accept that challenge, and fewer groups were willing to face that threat. The productivity of early OD efforts was limited. What was needed was a clear, descriptive, and systematic view of behavior and motivation.

My reading in the early sixties was largely in the field of sociology. I was particularly taken with Talcott Parsons and Neil Smelser's *Economy and Society*, in which the congruences between economic and social theory were identified and explored and in which individual behavior was seen as the basic element of the social process: "Every concrete act thus originates in a unit (member) and has effects on the system and its other component units. Hence these units constitute a system in the scientific sense that a change of state of any one will effect changes in the states of one or more others and thus of the system as a whole."

In 1951 Talcott Parsons joined with Edward Shils in editing a collection of papers entitled *Toward a General Theory of Action*, where they defined the personality as a system of action. Because I was familiar with a structural-functional approach to personality, Eric Berne's discussion of internal and external social and psychological advantages in his best-seller *Games People Play* struck me for its simplicity and clarity. It became a best-seller, I believe, because defining a behavioral transaction as the basic unit of investigation freed us from the ambiguities of the deductive approach. Berne assumed that by rigorous scrutiny of social transactions one could discover the universalities behind seemingly discrete behavior. Because the distance between apparently noncontinuous actions and the constructs which unify them is small, TA theory immediately appeals to the mind and can be empirically tested with relative ease. Behavior is, after all, an individual's fundamental tool for optimizing his life's possibilities. I am not surprised TA has reached the proportions of a mass movement.

Eric Berne was the seminal root from which many of the basic TA concepts sprang—games, strokes, ego states, script, and contract. The contribution of his colleagues he freely admitted. They helped him identify games and suggested catchy titles. In such a dynamic process it isn't always clear where one man's ideas leave off and another's begin, but I have attempted to give specific credit whenever I was able to discover it. I am confident that Berne, an innovator and a radical himself, would not have found unwelcome the eagerness with which others have reached for his ideas to extend the borders of human social control.

What I knew about transactional analysis in mid-1968 convinced me that TA might be the answer to the problems encountered in promoting OD. A training team that included Lyman Randall, Alan Mather, Fred Biamonte, and myself introduced it to clients and conducted our first public workshop in 1969. All of us went on to develop business applications of TA.

There are still people who remember the freshness of that first encounter with TA as they sat in a room filled with children's toys. Since then in hundreds of settings I have introduced behavior training to thousands in business. I have shared the relief of those who, liberated from the fears and games of the past, for the first time enjoy a sense of interpersonal competence. I have been impressed as organizations, now able to discuss their style and typical behavior, decide on new directions and accept significant goals for themselves. I have watched with quiet joy as people have permitted their real concerns to surface, enabling them to build new relationships based on mutual respect and interdependence.

The goal of our work is to help business organizations improve their integration and productivity because, in our view, individual health and effectiveness flow from and are secondary to the integration and productivity of a goal-oriented organization. With respect to this, our use of "behavior training" as a substitute for transactional analysis needs some explanation. "Process management" is our strategy for equipping managers with the theory and skills to understand and cope with the interpersonal dynamics of groups. "Corridor work" is used to help individuals understand how their behavior promotes or frustrates their own needs and goals as well as those of the organization. Important opportunities occur for managers to help others with their "personal" problems, and those behaviorally trained are well equipped to do this.

Giving interpersonal support is one of the challenges facing new-style managers; it is not the prerogative of only an elite few. Indeed, when the conspiracy to overlook behavior is exposed and individuals become aware of what's going on, their managers must be prepared to supply new levels of support. The willingness to move in that direction must exist before training begins. Individual agendas are not our primary concern except as they influence organizational health. Presumably something like this was on the minds of IBM corporate trainers when they decided to speak about "transactional emphasis" rather than transactional analysis.

This book is not so much to be read by managers as *used* by them as a tool to increase company vitality and individual self-awareness. It is a contribution to the effort of building better goal-achieving organizations. It owes much to my clients. They made it possible.

One of the joys of my work is in helping managers, where it is useful, to think again about their childhood. It is pleasant to reexperience the pains and glories of those early years from the position of concerned understanding. This involves the discovery that grown-ups are actually little boys and girls become large. My wife, Margaret Ann, and I have for the last ten years been expressing our interest in early childhood education in Happytime School in West Caldwell, New Jersey. Daily we enjoy the opportunity to grow with children of all ages. Some youngsters who have spent considerable time with us we have loved as our own children. Preschool is the most exciting field in education today bar none. Our attempts at introducing behavioral training into two public school systems have had moderate success, revealing that we still have a very long way to go.

In writing this book, my debt to friends who were eager to learn and to share is inestimable: Bill Burke, Dave Brown, Ted Clevenger, Noel Frizell, John Bromer, Mike Richards, Bill Luthy, Achille Giamara, Bill Langenstein, Joe Leidy, Cole Cooling, Ray Morse, Owen Quattlebaum, Dave Willcox, Jim Plastaras, Bob Miller, and Patsy Phillips.

Over the years I have used a multitude of resources from the behavioral sciences. Those familiar with the literature in the field will recognize my indebtedness, which I have attempted to record faithfully, especially in the bibliography and in the notes at the end of this book. After a number of years I reread with delight "P-A-C and Moral Values," the chapter usually attributed to Amy Harris in Tom Harris's book *I'm*

OK—You're OK. I recommend this thoughtful pericope to those who want to be fed on the "meat of the gospel."

The use of the third personal singular masculine pronoun in this book is a stylistic device and not a sexist statement.

I record here the contribution of my beloved wife, Margaret Ann. Those who enjoy the fruits of a long and productive marriage know how inadequately words report such things. Our children Paul, Martha, and Sarah contributed much joy and many opportunities to learn.

Dudley Bennett

contents

1

our three faces:
parent, adult, child

PEOPLE are not usually aware of how their behavior looks to others. Sometimes they wonder why they behave the way they do, but more often they wonder why *others* act as they do. To analyze behavior and its motivation, one must first understand that the basic component of behavior is an ego state. An ego state is a consistent combination of thought-feelings and related behavior. This means that our insides and outsides tend to be in synchronization.

Certain clusters of behavior always mean the same thing. A furrowed brow, angry eyes, and a pointing index finger have a clear meaning even if we don't hear the accompanying words, "You must never do that again." We can accurately conclude something about the individual's motivation whenever we see such behavior. To understand people, we must know two things about them—their characteristic behavior and the content of each ego state.

Each individual contains within himself three types of ego states. Parent ego states are imitations of parental figures. They reproduce feelings, attitudes, gestures, and concerns of historic people. Child ego states are surviving relics from infancy. They reproduce the feelings, behavior, and interpretations of a particular moment in the individual's childhood. Adult ego states function in the here-and-now and are concerned with collecting and computing data, estimating probabilities, and making decisions preparatory to action—all based on objective reality. The three states are summarized in Figure 1.

Members of the management team of an electronic component assembly plant studiously avoided talking with the plant head about relationships with corporate headquarters. The plant head—let us call him James Swansea—an otherwise reasonable and competent boss, would be thrown into a fit at the mention of corporate people and policies. He would become agitated, angry, and abusive. He accused corporate personnel of attempting to sabotage his career and of indifference to the plant and its people, and he became suspicious of subordinates he thought were friendly with headquarters. Team members found it easier to avoid the subject and keep a distance between themselves and headquarters rather than risk the boss's displeasure.

We have come to understand such a radical shift in behavior—from quiet, even-toned searching for answers to high-voiced, red-faced, angry aggressiveness—as a shift from one ego state to another. In the case of the plant manager, his energy flowed from his Adult to his Rebellious Child. When superiors did not behave in the fatherly way he expected, it provoked a burst of ill humor from him. His Child, we say, was "hooked."

Each type of ego state behavior arises from a different source, is self-experienced in a different way, and has different consequences for those around us. Shifts from one ego state to another represent not slight variations, but dramatic objective changes. It is not surprising, then, that a person sometimes seems to be not one individual but three. The identification of three kinds of ego states, their sources and consequences, and of alternative coping strategies is what structural analysis of behavior is about.

Ego states manifest themselves in two forms, either as fully turned on coherent behavior displays, which the actor identifies as the "real self," or as intrusions or interruptions into current ego state activities. Eruptions from a latent ego state may occur below the actor's level of awareness, which, along

Personality Structure	Parent Ego State	Adult Ego State	Child Ego State
Concept of life	Taught concept of life: "How to" lists, rights and wrongs. Source of quick evaluative judgments.	Thought concept of life: Center of (1) data processing; (2) probability estimating; (3) decision-making.	Felt concept of life: source and seat of emotions.
Basic concern	To be right, to be "on target."	To be respected as competent, recognized as good decision-maker.	To be liked.
Special attributes	Storehouse of standards of social controls and emotional norms, lists of "shoulds" and "should nots"—conscience.	Only data processor in here-and-now, awareness of no certainty for success, only some degree of probability for success or failure.	Wants immediate results, guarantees and certainties, instant gratification—vastly more willing to receive than to give.

Figure 1. Structure of the personality.

with other evidence, demonstrates that an individual can be in two or three ego states at one time.*

A useful way to understand ego states and their relation to each other is to conceptualize them as organs of the psyche connected with semipermeable membranes. They are energized at a certain level. (1) Energy can be inactive and bound in an ego state, unable to directly influence behavior. When energy is repressed, or excluded, it remains only as latent potential. (2) Energy can be unbound and exhibited as uncontrolled motion. In that state, energy is kinetic, and it is relatively difficult to move kinetic energy across ego state boundaries. (3) Energy can be directed by choice. Thus "free" energy, sometimes called muscular energy, can move easily across ego state boundaries. It is what I consciously regard as "me." The ego state where free energy dominates is perceived by the individual to be his "real self."

The ego state that has executive power over the personality is the one in which free plus unbound energy predominates. When Swansea acted out overly angry opposition to headquarters, free energy from his Adult had joined the unbound energy from his Child, which took over as executive of the personality.

We can isolate three factors which govern psychic energy shifts: environmental forces acting on each state, permeability of boundaries between ego states, and the energy level of each state. Once Swansea understood his behavior, he strove to maintain more free energy in his Adult when his Child was hooked. Later, after much practice, he was able to face stressful problems with superiors without regressing to infant rebellion and attack. His stabilized Adult could remain the executive in the face of strong restimulations of the Parent or Child.

Diagnosis of ego states. There are four forms of diagnosis for understanding what motivates an individual. The primary one is the skill to scrutinize behavior clues that the actor exhibits. Behavior reveals far more about what an individual is up to in social situations than most managers realize. No be-

* The chapter on how the personality functions in Eric Berne's *Transactional Analysis in Psychotherapy* discusses this topic in some detail.

havior is without meaning. Clear understanding of behavioral concepts plus keen observation can tell a great deal about the actor's intentions—even things he may not be aware of himself. Objective diagnosis considers facial expressions, voice tones, vocabulary, posture, gestures, and the overall impression summed up in concept of life, basic concerns, and special attributes (as shown in Figure 1).

A second and more precarious form of diagnosis is the observation of the consequences of an individual's transactions with others in a social situation. If people characteristically respond to individual A with compliance or rebellion, we may tentatively conclude that they are under the influence of A's Parent ego state. If people characteristically respond to individual B in a motherly or fatherly way, we may conclude that B is offering childlike stimuli. If respondents appear calm and ask questions of C, revealing the presence of their active intelligence, we may conclude that C is in his Adult ego state.

Conversely, if worker A and worker B are repairing a leaky tank, and A says in his Adult, "Hand me the torch," B's reply will reveal his operant ego state. If B says: "Be damned careful with that thing," we presume his response comes from his Parent. If he says: "Do you want the wide nozzle?" we assume he is in his Adult. If he says peevishly: "I don't think you could do without me around here," we diagnose his complaint as arising from his Child.

Subjective diagnosis, the third form, occurs when, for example, we ask a person which ego state he is in and he responds, "I feel angry at how the company treats me." From reports of his inner activity, we are able to deduce the operant ego state. The accuracy of the deduction depends on the individual's ability to recognize and identify his feelings with minimum distortion. If on reflection he finds he is acting as he remembers his father acting in 1935, we identify Parent behavior. If he observes his feelings to be reenactments of sentiments he first experienced in Paducah, Kentucky, before he was 5 years old, he is in his Child.

Since personality, like a house, is built from the foundation up, any factual information about a person's childhood will be useful in understanding his present behavior. This is historical diagnosis, the fourth form. Pertinent facts might relate to family members, their integration and cultural values, the relative benignity of rearing practices, and particular environmental factors, such as education, geography, and politics.

Historical and subjective diagnosis cannot be made under ordinary business circumstances. The manager is usually limited to behavioral and social diagnosis. The more of these forms used, however, the sounder the diagnosis will be.

The expense account is one management area that often stimulates rather dramatic displays of ego states. A cloth goods salesman's behavior astonished his peers. At times he would handle his out-of-pocket account with a matter-of-fact reality that reflected both his company's concern for frugality and his appreciation of its useful potential for closing a sale. At other times his expense sheet would be swollen with myriad expenses that strained credibility. When someone from the finance department would phone him, his response would be fiercely querulous and petty. On still other occasions his tab sheets were remarkably lean, suggesting that he was absorbing costs that could be legitimately charged to the company.

After behavior training, he was able to identify that his bloated account was a surviving relic of the carefree way he had viewed money as a little boy. It had always been there. He'd had but to ask for it. He recognized the stoic attitude of his father when his expenses reflected less than actual costs. He had ingested his father's concern to "be his own man," to "go it alone." Gradually he was able to understand and discriminate between his rebellious Child, his (relatively) unrealistic Parent, and his more effective Adult. By deliberately putting his Adult in charge on this matter, he benefited from reduced unpleasantness in his relations with finance and a general improvement in his overall effectiveness. This is one of the benefits of structural analysis: managers can modify their own behavior to make it more congruent with their own Adult-verified goals.

The Parent Ego State

Sometimes referred to by Berne as the "exterior ego state," the Parent is a huge collection of attitudes, feelings, and ideas of others incorporated uncritically into the personality. You've heard the hackneyed: "Never discuss sex, politics, or religion in polite company because you're sure to get into trouble." The reason for this is that people often hold these most important aspects of life in their Parent. It is belief and behavior received whole from parental figures or institutions and assumed to be true without either investigation or evidence. On subjects like these, parents tend to speak in sepulchral tones. Indeed they may reinforce their position by quoting divinity in their behalf. Because we were first given these "truths" when our parents were, for all practical purposes, gods, there is little chance that we could have received them with critical awareness.

One might assume that as biological aging takes place, positions arbitrarily accepted during the dependency of childhood would be tested against reality by emerging and growing intelligence for their appropriateness in the here-and-now. Unfortunately, individuals often allow areas of personality to exist outside the purview of reason, surviving as archaic rigidities and prejudices from the past. These remain intact possibly because no occasion presented itself as an opportunity to test assumptions and ideas long familiar if not friendly. Since childhood is generally assumed to be the happiest time of life, when we were closer to simplicity and truth, old ideas are held inviolate. It takes a great amount of psychic energy to set things right. If there is no reward for this and people around us only applaud devotion to the past—well, it just seems easier and more pleasant to go along with them. A great benefit of structural analysis is that a clear path can be pointed out to those who desire something better.

We tend to forget that a very large part of our social structuring was recorded without editing from the external environment before we had the benefits of reason. The basic molding took place before the emergence of infant intelligence. Unlike other species which relatively soon after birth can survive without continuous parent protection, the human infant goes through an extended period of dependency.

The gestation period of the human fetus is only half completed at birth. The second half takes place outside the womb. This has a number of important consequences. One is that during the fundamental days and months of life, the infant has no reason. He cannot understand in the usual sense what's happening to him. He has no words or logic at his disposal. He can't compare this experience with any other to make interpretations and judgments. And, of course, he is helpless to effect change. If hungry, he can't feed himself, or if cold, he can't seek a blanket. If frightened, he can't ask for consolation. This radical dependency seems to be the price of future autonomy. It also powerfully contributes to lifelong patterns of obedience and acquiescence.

The Parent state contains a multitude of cautions, warnings, rules, and laws that have been collected from the Parent states of other people. It contains all the things ingested from parent figures from earliest admonitions heard only as unintelligible sounds or judgments expressed by more or less indifferent nursing. It is reinforced with facial expressions and the presence or absence of hugging. These same values are later expressed as "do's" and "don'ts," "oughts" and "musts." Bombarded with these all our life, we tend to internalize them and later to define ourselves by them. Breach of this structuring causes guilt, shame, and that most painful human emotion—embarrassment.

While Parent material seems mostly negative, it can also contain moments of pleasure, joy, and fulfillment recorded when parents were playful and caring. Much Parent material is of the "how to" variety and it helps things go along easily and in fashion. It teaches

How to talk with superiors.
How to eat soup.
How to give a party.
How to dress for the office.
How to treat animals.
How to groom your hair.
How to order dinner.

When we realize how many of these rules there are, we begin to comprehend the impressive size of the Parent in our heads. And since the rules were fortified with strong words such as "always" or "never," it is almost impossible for the average person to breach them. An amusing but telling report is told of a sociology class whose members found themselves incapable of singing the first verse of *America* out loud while riding the subway home from school. The instructor's amusement turned to chagrin when he discovered himself also bound by the same inner controls. Few of us realize the strength of the controls represented by the internalized Parent.

As young children, we begin to receive more complex material from other parental figures:

Believe in God.
My country right or wrong.
Birds of a feather flock together.
Truth will out.
Blood will tell.
Waste not, want not.
You can never trust a woman (a man).
If you don't take care of yourself, no one else will.
Always forgive, never forget.
Good fences make good neighbors.

The list is endless. Parent dictums seem to make a lot of sense, particularly when pronounced with either an assertive or a helpless tone of voice. Unfortunately, closer inspection reveals they may make little or no sense at all in terms of immediate realities. Yet universally they pass as accepted truth. A significant organizational pathology is revealed when people blindly accept Parent statements as accurate descriptions of reality. The skill to detect Parent material and to understand its archaic nature is as important to the manager as is his ability to reason. Parent material may pass as knowledge and competence to the casual observer, but a closer look often reveals its low substantive content.

Parent material will often be contradictory, inconsistent, and confusing. Since, in our culture, punishing mistakes is far more common than rewarding accomplishments, Parent material is often received amid the shame and confusion of ineptness or failure. Parents do not strive for consistency. Saying one thing while acting out another seems not to be a source of concern to parents, who may remain indifferent and unclear about certain beliefs and behaviors all their lives. Some people respond to inadequate and contradictory parenting by decommissioning their own Parent. "Your values," they say, "are not relevant," "Everything is relative," or "When they all get together and decide what the rules are, I'll live by them." Seeking to escape the hard work of discovery and definition, they contend either that they have no values or that the whole subject is meaningless. Even more serious, they surrender value considerations to superiors and applaud themselves on their ability to follow orders.

Much organizational mischief arises when managers are underpowered in their Parent ego state. Watergate happened in part because senior officials lacked appreciation of the functional nature of values. Faced with the alternative of changing leaders or values, happily the republic opted for the prior. Managers with a weakened Parent are unable to take a stand with conviction. They waffle and drift. In place of self-definition, we find opportunism which accepts leadership that is merely fashionable or financially rewarding. Strengthening the intelligence in TA means much more than thinking clearly. It also means allowing oneself to be appropriately emotional and to hold values that maximize the possibilities of social life.

The desire to avoid making the effort to define and live the ethical life is ill conceived and counterproductive for healthy companies and people. The question is not whether to have values, but what the values of the individual and the organization are and how they influence each other. The TA-trained manager takes the time to identify his company's assumptions and values relating to work, people, quality, attitude, profit, and dealings with other organizations. These values are measured in the light of relevant traditions and most recent developments in human resource utilization. Then they become part of management decision-making. The Japanese are clearly in the lead in understanding the contribution of values to organizational integration and individual motivation. Operating factories as modern as tomorrow without violating ethical principles as old as their civilization, they have wrought an industrial miracle since the Second World War. In this area we have much to learn from them.

At this point a distinction which often causes confusion must be clarified. The Parent has two functional modes, either as a fully active ego state or as an internal influence. Saying the Parent ego state is active means our Parent is talking now. That is, your mother or father or other parental figure is speaking through you. Acting under parental influence means your Child is talking that way to please your Parent. You are behaving as your mother or father wished you to. Compliance and obedience show the influence of the internalized Parent. The supervisor who is deferential and docile when dealing with the department head shows his internal Parent influence. When he displays control, suspicion, and anger toward subordinates, his Parent ego state is functioning.

The Parent is sometimes referred to as an "electrode" because of its characteristic quick response and often high discharge. Our Parent is talking or influencing us when we find ourselves stubbornly holding on to a position we probably wouldn't mind giving up if we were in the Adult ego state.

Observation of Parent behavior reveals that it has two quite different modes of expression—nurturing and judging (Figure

	Nurturing	Judgmental
Thoughts	Work hard Do your best Everything will be OK Don't worry Never give up Stiff upper lip	Do/Don't Good/Bad Always/Never Ought I know best Right/Wrong Must
Feelings	Protective Loving Encouraging	Self-righteous Intolerant Demanding
Behavior	Smiling Outstretched arms Concerned look Hugging	Foot-tapping Furrowed brow Head-wagging Stern stare Finger-wagging. Hands on hips

Figure 2. Parent ego state.

2). The nurturing side is solicitous, sympathetic, and supportive. Characteristic behavior is hugging, reaching for, protecting, and smiling. When we exhibit automatic support behavior, we reveal the content of our parental training. To reach
spontaneously for the fallen does not necessarily arise from
thought or feeling. Some people are made that way.

The punishing or judgmental side is seen in the Punishing
Parent manager who, whether right or wrong, is always certain.
Characteristic behavior is taunting, accusing, and criticizing.
The person in this state assumes that his position is right and
that there is nothing to discuss. Acquiescence is demanded.
"See things the way I see them" is the proffered contract. This
person is hard-working, domineering, authoritarian, and
moralistic, and tends to treat others as children.

Parent-dominant types like to see themselves as rescuing
others and may take professional roles to further this activity.
They are most quickly recognized by the judgmental tone of
their voice even though the words may be Adult. Relying on
slogans, they discourse in pious generalities often accompanied with frowns and disapproving looks. Their vocabulary
is liberally sprinkled with "oughts" and "musts." The material
for this position often dates back to the forgotten past. Any
behavior that indicates one is closed to new data or makes
automatic judgments based on archaic material reveals the
judgmental Parent ego state.

Our basic concern when we are in our Parent is to be
"right," to be "on target," to be "true to our traditions." The
Parent is the source of our quick evaluative judgments. It is the
storehouse of emotional norms and standards for social control.
It contains the "how to" lists and the "shoulds" and "should
nots." It is often referred to as the conscience. It guides us
toward what is perceived as right and away from what is perceived as wrong. The insistent behavior arises not so much out
of substantive validity as imitation of parents or their surrogates. "We've done it this way for ten years, and I don't intend
to change it now" sounds reasonable, but it may also be a
cover-up of serious problems. This can be determined only by
scrutiny of the pros and cons of the position. The point is that
Parent assurance in itself may be sense or nonsense.

The functioning Parent conserves energy since it handles

much ordinary behavior automatically. It also reduces anxiety related to decision-making, and to the degree that its pre-set patterns represent the patterns of the larger society, the Parent helps things to go smoothly. It can also be a lifesaver by evoking automatic responses in times of stress and danger. Of course, when old answers don't work, automatic responses are counterproductive. New data may change the problem, or unusual circumstances may intervene. The manager who is not free to question or test solutions and attempt to construct new alternatives becomes part of the problem instead of part of the solution. Understanding structural analysis is the first step in freeing managers from this deadly trap.

The Child Ego State

Usually considered the most important of the three, the Child ego state contains those aspects of personality which are not shared by other individuals. Genuine historical people and events constitute our Child ego state. It contains emotions, attitudes, and interpretations, and their concomitant behaviors, of what we saw, heard, felt, and understood in earliest years (Figure 3). It reproduces the behavior and mental state at a particular time in our development, using, of course, grown-ups' resources. Grown-ups' demonstrations of frustration, anger, and pleasure are reminiscent of infant behavior.

Whereas the Parent contains accumulated external data, the Child contains the internal responses made during early life cycle stages. It is hard to imagine what goes on in the mind of the young child before reason and the ability to use symbols emerged. We conclude from observation that there are feelings plus adaptations and interpretations of infant experiences. As in the case of the Parent, current transactions recreate childhood situations and have the power to restimulate the feelings we had then. When our Child is restimulated today, we reexperience the same emotions we first experienced as a child, and we interpret present events in the same way we interpreted these events the first time we experienced them. The individual's past behavior is transferred to and expressed in the present.

Current events may "hook" our Child and cause a replay of stored feelings. Not being invited to a party can hook bad

	ADAPTIVE		NATURAL
	Compliant Child	Rebellious Child	
Thoughts	Don't leave me Love me Help me Show me Protect me	No I won't Never	I want I wish I can Let me
Feelings	Insecure Dependent Fearful Cautious Affectionate	Frustration Anger Rebellion	Insecure Fun-loving Affectionate Curious Inventive Rebellious
Behavior	Compliant Wringing hands Cowering Downcast eyes Biting lip Biting nails	Tantrum Attack Sulking Pouting Withdrawal	Laughter Pleading Play Tears Touching Watchful Anger

Figure 3. Child ego state.

feelings related to rejection during early socialization experiences. Forgotten by friends or relatives, we may reexperience feelings of abandonment that we first knew in the cradle. Facing present unfriendly alternatives, we may reexperience the powerlessness we first knew as infants. This explains why a seemingly minor event can cause great uneasiness or a small matter stimulate a profound emotional discharge. It hooks our whole load of negative feelings about ourselves. If an observer did not know where it was coming from, a dramatic display of shouting, angry gesturing, and livid coloring, all caused by a minor incident, might cause him to conclude that the actor had "flipped his wig." In fact, this is a natural process whereby stored hurts accumulate until we "explode." While not pleasant, it is preferable to the alternatives.

Rather obviously, what we are dealing with here is not

memory. The term "reliving" better explains the behavior. We do not simply remember what we felt as a child. We have the same feelings now. "There never was such a thing as a happy childhood," Thomas Harris said from a platform we once shared. The happy childhood is one of those unexamined myths maintained by selective recall.*

To understand the source and power of the NOT OK most people labor under, we have to remind ourselves of the radical helplessness of our infant years. The tiny child has urges to explore his body and his environment, to touch, bang, taste, make sounds, soil himself, and experience the joy of discovery. At the same time he is confronted with myriad uncompromising demands to surrender this natural behavior in exchange for parental approval. In absolute need of parental affective support mainly in the form of constant body contact, he discovers it is often withheld or conditional. It is given most satisfactorily only when parental demands are met. Very early then the association is set—painful loneliness can best be assuaged by meeting parental demands. Thus societal values are bargained for and primal patterns of obedience fostered in return for parental affection.

Often we find it too difficult to learn to understand and cope with feelings of rejection, abandonment, and loneliness arising out of early childhood experiences. It is easier to deny or repress them. Instead of bringing them to the surface and working them through with our Adult and freeing ourselves from old fears, we turn the feelings off. We replace spontaneity with self-consciousness, and authenticity (genuineness) with adaptation. Rather than struggle for self-definition, we seek leaders who will protect and support our Child and Parent ego states. We seek new parent figures to replace the old. We "go along." Obedience to father, fatherland, and fatherlike leaders becomes a virtue. Child-dominant managers tend either to be compliant and to meet expectations or to be withdrawn and fail to fulfill expectations. Don't look to them for initiative, clear-thinking, and responsible follow-through.

The infant's day is defined by the relative proximity of the

---

* Harris enlarges on this in Chapters 2 and 3 of his best-selling *I'm OK—You're OK*.

parents. If they approach, he can be cuddled, stroked, nourished, cleaned, and played with. If they withdraw, his world soon becomes diminished. It goes back to zero, awaiting the benevolence of their return. This in-and-out motion and the associated experience of pleasure and pain results in an accumulated deposit of negative feelings which leads the child to make the feeling-decision (adaptation) about himself "I'm not OK." That is, when you approach me, good things happen to me and I am restored; therefore I conclude that you are OK and the possible source of my well-being.

Civilized life is frustrating to the human infant because of the necessary and lengthy intermediation of the parent. The consequence of this constant thwarting of basic urges is accumulated negative feelings in the child. This is what led Harris to conclude that "there never was such a thing as a happy childhood," its glories due far more to selective memory than inherent joys. Parental patterns are reinforced daily in children, which leads most of us to experience our remaining days through the lens of the NOT OK Child.

The basic assumption that most people are victims of more or less benign rearing practices and are burdened with NOT OK feelings from early childhood is fundamental to the formulation of managerial strategies to develop sound organizations and healthy people. Claude Steiner and others see Harris's idea of NOT OK as a departure from Berne. Berne held that people are perfectly alright the way they are. The task is not to change them but, with adequate nurturing, to let them become what they essentially are—OK. Harris seems to say that although rearing practices, social norms, and historical and environmental factors are important influences, the NOT OK condition is primarily the residue of simply being a child. No one disputes that nearly everyone has such a life position, whatever its source. The presence of the NOT OK Child can be identified when we withdraw and sulk, or aggress and punish; or when we show signs of distress such as weeping, teasing, blushing, tearing, yawning.

The Child is the felt concept of life. It is the source and seat of human emotions. When we are in our Child, our major concern is to be liked. Our Child wants immediate, plentiful gratification, and he doesn't want it to stop. He wants instant results, guarantees, and certainties. Unwilling to defer gratification, the Child in us is unable or unwilling to invest in the long term; instead he seizes the immediate. In general, our Child

Directs attention toward himself.
Goes on the defensive.
Feels disapproved of.
Accepts negative judgments about himself.
Constantly says "I ought" or "I have to."
Is fearful of being wrong.
Follows instructions resentfully.
Is playful, irresponsible, and competitive.
Has an unrealistic negative self-image.
Is more willing to receive than to give.

There is another side of our Child. The first great discoveries about himself and life bring joy and excitement. The touch of mother's skin and of soft, fuzzy things. The pleasure of oral feeding and that great sensation of being half-asleep and half-awake. Romping with friendly animals. The fun of the holidays. The big feelings when listening to martial music. The heady experience of a warm spring day with luscious colors and smells. The fun of playing in a puddle and discovering the wondrous uses of mud. The satisfaction of eating food that runs down the chin. Enjoyment of friends next door, picnics, baseball, swimming, and lots of hugs from the family. However, my continuous observation of preschoolers and grown-ups has led to the belief that in most individuals NOT OK experiences are more numerous than OK experiences.

What I have been describing was called by Berne the Natural Child. Our Natural Child has potentially available all the natural feelings that can occur within us as a consequence of our transactions with the environment. This is the way a baby behaves—he is impulsive, curious, self-centered, and affectionate when his needs are met and angry when they are not. Because his responses are an authentic expression of his feelings, we describe him as *transparent*. Our Natural Child has a full spectrum of built-in feelings that he will exhibit in response to the environment. Here is one of the many possible classifications of the Natural Child's affects—his visible, consciously experienced emotions:

Positive Feelings	Less Positive Feelings
Joy	Shame
Surprise	Sorrow
Sympathy	Fear
Trust	Chagrin
Hope	Anger
Benignity	Guilt
Love	Anxiety

There is, however, another dimension to the affective side of behavior. As a result of powerful socializing forces of parents and institutions, our natural feelings become skewed and patterned to agree with the pre-set ideas of society—"Men don't cry," "Soft feelings are feminine," "Intimacy breeds contempt," "When men, like steel, lose their temper, they're no good," "Always forgive, never forget," "Never let on when they get to you," "Obedience is necessary."

For most of us, the Adaptive Child has almost completely supplanted the Natural Child. Our feelings are stylized and ritualized, produced on demand for those who taught us to feel good or bad about what they valued. Those who have known the soldier's sense of fulfillment at having passed Saturday morning inspection with spit-shined boots, shining brass buckle, and a steam-cleaned rifle will recognize their adaptive side. So too will those who think a woman dressed up like a rabbit is sexy.

The Adaptive Child is our socialized feelings that occur as a consequence of our having internalized parental training. You see him when an employee accepts blame and punishment from a manager without a discussion of what the employee did wrong and how he can do better next time, and particularly when the employee exhibits shame and guilt. He is responding to the Punishing Parent, as he has done many times before. Chances are that both people in this transaction will consider this to be proper behavior. The same manager would be properly submissive when receiving similar treatment from his boss. In the first instance the manager demonstrates his Punishing Parent, in the second, his Adaptive Child.

The Adaptive Child has learned to avoid pain and to gain approval. He has internalized "proper" values and feelings in order to survive. Instead of acting spontaneously, the Adaptive Child reacts to internalized parents. In place of authenticity is adaptation. The Adaptive Child looks for a savior and plays the game "Gee, I Wish . . ." or "Bad Things Always Seem to Happen to Me." These activities take the place of problem-solving.

Another noteworthy aspect of Child behavior, referred to in the literature as the "Little Professor," is the smart-alec Child who figures things out on his own. He is innately intuitive, creative, and manipulative—an artist at getting his own way. This kind of manager "flies by the seat of his pants," eschewing systematic approaches to decision-making. He admits he doesn't know how he does it, but things seem to work out for him. In another setting he is a con man who seems to have the uncanny ability to always land on his feet. He uses intuition to psych out situations.

If you have seen a man repeatedly charm a room full of peers with his self-deprecating stories, or watched a woman walk across a room in such a way that all heads turn, you have seen the Little Professor. His charm worked for him when he was very young and it has worked ever since. However, as a situation increases in complexity, the Little Professor is less viable and more prone to wrong decisions and erroneous conclusions.

We emerge from childhood, then, with a set of internalized opinions and related behaviors plus a stylized arrangement of feelings that remain an intact, powerful influence throughout life. This explains why there is so much inappropriate, unproductive company behavior. While the behavior may appear to come from and deal with the present, in fact it is material from infancy replayed in grown-up garb. What is that 2-year-old up to? is the question that comes to mind when observing these transactions.

The Adult Ego State

The engineer at a metal stamping plant spent most of his time in his office, developing work flow charts, linear programs, and confidence limits from work sampling studies collected by subordinates. About one-third of his time was spent in meetings or on the shop floor. He reported he had "dog days," when he felt tense, downcast, and irritable. Experience had taught him that in order to improve his concentration, he should spend such days in his office away from people, where his irritability was less likely to get him into trouble with others. He avoided facing big problems or making decisions on "one of those days." On other days he found his office rather confining, and enjoyed rubbing shoulders on the floor with other employees and "gassing" with subordinates. When he was in his upbeat mood, lunch hour often stretched to two, as did the martinis, after which he would return to the office like a boy going whimpering to the dentist.

Because his performance was appraised as mediocre, he matter-of-factly questioned the personnel officer: "Do you think my behavior patterns are working against me?" His reflective tone of voice indicated that he was not expecting an answer. He bemusedly commented that his behavior changes reminded him of another person who exhibited rather dramatic changes leaping in and out of phone booths.

Let's interrupt our story to note that one of the benefits of the behavioral approach to management is that in a very short time an employee can gain sufficient understanding of where he is and what options are open to him so that he can soon begin to make behavior adjustments. He doesn't need to know everything about himself, just that piece of information that moves him off center and creates momentum toward improvement. When he gets his life back under control, there is often an immediate payoff in reduction of anxiety and release of new energy and hope. Later, when new problems are confronted or the individual is ready to undertake new learnings, more pieces can be added to the puzzle. Since many behavior problems arise out of simple lack of understanding of the elements of transactions, many managers enjoy significant short-

range improvement by correcting misconceptions of the consequences of their behavior on others.

The personnel officer told the plant engineer that when he
retreated to his office and focused entirely on paper work, his
Adaptive Child was responding to the stern dictums: "Be the
best," "Take care of old number one," and "Trust no one." His
impulsive, gratification-seeking Natural Child was displayed
in his "Oh, what the hell" behavior at lunch. And when he
matter-of-factly described his own behavior and compared
himself to Superman–Clark Kent, he was in his Adult ego
state. He was aware of and reflecting on current realities.

In addition to accounting for the plant engineer's three
ego states and relating them to the engineer's behavior,
the personnel officer explained to him that the Adult
was the only one capable of here-and-now behavior. This
caught the plant engineer's interest—it hooked his Adult.
He asked questions about how to "turn off the Child and turn
on the Adult" and what books he could use to build on his
meager knowledge. From that beginning his behavior
changed and there was real improvement in his ability to
communicate with others in the shop. As his understanding of
his own and others' behavior grew—his understanding of Parent, Adult, and Child ego states—the personnel officer was
able to help him face and solve problems of increasing difficulty. He reported that he experienced greater comfort and reduced social estrangement, which contributed to increased
effectiveness.

The Adult ego state (Figure 4) functions like a computer. It
is used for processing data, estimating probabilities, and making decisions as a basis for action. It develops the thought
concept of life. Experiences are processed into useful pieces of
information, compared with what is already known, and filed
in the storage area of like information. Material so processed
can be retrieved for future use. The Adult is the only ego state
that functions in what is called "real time" or the "here-and-
now." Whereas the Parent is rigid and judgmental, enforcing
the standards of others, and the prelogical Child reacts on the
basis of distorted archaic sentiments, the Adult computes
present-time information into decisions.

The Adult is not related to age in the life cycle. Its ability to

Thoughts	Who? What? Why? When? Where? Executive between Child and Parent Develops alternatives Estimates probabilities Makes decisions
Feelings	Feelings are transferred from the Child to the Adult via the emancipated Adult. No longer out of the past, these feelings are reality-based, direct, and authentic. Some argue that there is no anger in the Adult.
Behavior	Active concerned listening Pondering and reflective Patient and relaxed Head squared on both horizontal and vertical planes Large muscle activity

Figure 4. Adult ego state.

function depends on the amount of work it gets. Like any organ, it can atrophy through disuse or become stronger with exercise. When we are in our Adult, our attention is directed to what can be known about the real world. Our basic Adult concern is to be respected for the quality of our actions as competent decision-makers. Since, for the Adult, manipulation of objective data is important, it often asks such questions as "Who?" "What?" and "Why?" The Adult is aware of no certainty for success, but of some degree of probability for success or failure. In general, the Adult

Directs attention to the here-and-now problem.
Describes.
Seeks to understand the situation.
Attempts to identify causal factors.
Analyzes.
Asks, Is this the best way?
Compares alternatives.

Is confident and nondefensive.

Is reality-oriented.

During infancy, our Adult intelligence may be weak and overcome by fears in the Child and commands in the Parent. But since the Adult is potentially more powerful than the other two, it can, with understanding and serious effort, not only survive but prevail against the contamination of both of the other states. It can become the executive of the personality.

Synthesis

Once we are able to differentiate the "three persons" within us, we are able to make great improvements in problem analysis. Any business issue can be handled from any of the three ego states. Each state simply has a different consequence. In general, the Parent says, "There is no problem I can't apply my answers to"; the Child says, "There's no problem so big I can't run away from it"; and the Adult asks, "What are the facts?"

The Adult is able to turn the three-part division to advantage. In any problem it has three sources of information: the content of both Parent and Child ego states plus the present reality. The Adult carefully lays out the content of its Parent state and decides whether or not it is true and examines it with regard to its applicability to the present situation. It seeks to identify the feelings of the Child to establish their suitability. It also uses itself to discover what information the objective environment gives about the problem. When this process is employed, the Adult becomes the executive of the personality. The goal is not to do away with the Parent and the Child—life would be dull and brutish without them—but to first clarify and then compare these important sources of information.

Twenty supervisors in a knitting mill were asked for their opinions regarding the behavior of one of their members (supervisor A). Supervisor A had been with the company for 20 years. In the last 24 months he had been almost totally ineffective and frequently under the influence of alcohol. People around him tended to feel sorry or angry about the situation and hoped something would cause him to change. The other supervisors had overlooked the problem for some time because of A's long service, but the day had arrived when they felt something had to be done. When the supervisors were confronted with the problem at a meeting, they decided to apply the Parent-Adult-Child (P-A-C) problem analysis model. This meant finding out the Parent opinions and the Child feelings of group members toward supervisor A and the necessary factual (Adult) information. Results of their analysis were as follows:

PARENT OPINIONS

No work, no pay.
We expect more, not less, from older employees.
You can never change a drunk.
You don't have to like work—just do it.
No one in this company gets special treatment.
Who does he think he is?
One bad apple can spoil the whole barrel.

CHILD FEELINGS

Frustration: Why does he do this? Doesn't he care about his family? ". . . and after all the things the company has done for him."
Anger: We have to obey the rules, and so does he.
Sympathy: I wonder what's going on with his wife and kids.
Hope: Operator six says he's been doing better lately.
Secret pleasure: Better him than me.
Failure: I've never been able to help this kind. It's too much for me.
Pessimism: It gets us all sooner or later.
Escape: It's best to leave an individual's problems alone. It will only make things worse if we get involved.

INFORMATION SOUGHT BY ADULT

What resources do we have in the company to help him?
What is the real problem behind the symptomatic drinking?
Has he been to a doctor?
Does he talk about the problem?
Is the situation stable or deteriorating?

How is the production in his department?
How close is he to retirement?
Is there something about the plant that bugs him?
Who are his friends? Who does he talk to?
Can personnel people help?

The issue could be handled from any of the three ego states. A manager can accuse and blame; he can retreat and look the other way, hoping for a miracle; or he can search for causes and identify possible solutions. Each state, by itself, has very different consequences. It is interesting to note in this instance that Parent sloganeering not only isn't helpful but probably makes matters worse. The Parent is some distance from the problem and moving further away. The Child, if supportive, offers some real possibility for help but probably only if it is linked to the Adult. We do not necessarily conclude that the best decisions are made by the Adult. But when the Adult processes data from the other ego states as well as from itself, we expect the best outcomes. Further benefits of this process are that it liberates and elevates rationality, and over time strengthens Adult intelligence.

The information in Figure 5 suggests how elements of behavior related to each ego state indicate which state an individual is likely to be coming from. Although 100 percent certainty about which ego state is operative isn't possible, we can be close enough for most purposes. Distinguishing between Punishing Parent and Rebellious Child is the most difficult. The more clues we consider, the more confidence we can have in our judgment.

(Figure 5 is on pages 26–27.)

Figure 5. Behavioral clues indicating which psychological state is at work.

Divisions or Basic Norms	Nurturing Parent	Punishing Parent	Adult Ego State	Natural Child	Adaptive Child
Voice tones	Solicitous, comforting, caring, soothing.	Condescending, criticizing, putting down or accusing, taut, insistent, tongue-clicking, sighing.	Matter-of-fact, even, calm.	Rising, high-pitched, usually noisy.	Whining, shrieking with rage, begging, contrite, supplicating.
Vocabulary clues	What's wrong? Are you OK? Can I help? Don't worry. Everything will be OK.	Shocking. Nonsense. Lazy. Poor thing. Everyone knows that. You should never. The only way. I can't understand why in the world you would ever. It is extremely important. Do it. You never.	How? What? When? Where? Why? Who? What's the probability? Is it possible? Is it probable? In what way? I speak only for myself and not others.	I'm mad at you. Hey, great. I wish. I dunno. Gee, crazy. Rats. Wow.	It always happens to me. I guess I'm just unlucky. I never seem to win at anything. That's not fair. Everybody else does it. Come on, let's. I won't.
Physical postures	Open arms protecting from a fall or hurt, pat on back, arm around shoulder.	Stroking chin, puffed up, super correct, very proper. Superior attitudes: talking behind hand, throwing hands in air.	Relaxed, attentive, eye contact, listening with openness, squared-up posture. Adult listening is identified with continual movement of face, eyes, and body.	Playful, excited, running, dancing, jumping up and down, head cocked.	Withdrawn and retreating, beat down, overburdened, self-conscious, teasing, agitated, tantrum behavior.

Facial expressions	Concerned, supportive, encouraging, warm, happy.	Frowns, worried or disapproving looks, taut lips, jutting chin, stern gaze.	Alert eyes, paying close attention.	Excitement, surprise, eyes shining, body tense, mouth open.	Downcast eyes, quivering lip or chin, tic, pouting, whining, moist eyes, red face.
Gestures	Reaching for, hugging, holding, protecting and shielding from harm.	Pointing index finger or pencil, tapping foot, arms folded across chest, hands on hips, striking table with fist, shaking fist.	Leaning forward in chair, eye-to-eye contact, listening with openness.	Laughter, limbs moving freely, playful.	Wringing hands, withdrawing into corner, raising hand for permission, stopped shoulders, hung head.
General	Support and concern.	Closure to new data, automatic judgments based on archaic material.	Data gathering, sensitivity, openness, and thinking.	Aroused feelings suggesting that the Child has been hooked.	Complaining and expectation-meeting, or withdrawing and expectation-avoiding.

2

a social theory of communication

IN ADDITION to being a model of personality and a mode of therapy, transactional analysis is a theory of communication. At the heart of TA is an investigative method of analyzing transactions between people by breaking them down into their component ego states. A transaction is a basic unit of social intercourse. It consists of an exchange of words and behavior between two people. Conversation usually means an oral exchange of words and sounds. Communication can mean only that, or it may also include written and visual symbols. Transaction is larger than both conversation and communication. It includes all forms of contact between people: social and psychological, material and spiritual.

When one person directs communication toward another, the gambit contains an implied expectation of how the other person will respond, whether they are aware of it or not. When A approaches B, A makes assumptions of where B is and subtly, subliminally suggests, by the way he addresses him, how B is to respond (that is, which ego state). From one point of view, doing well in business is the consequence of successfully meeting the expectations of others who transact with us. From the other side, the ability to select the appropriate ego state from which to transact markedly enhances our chances of getting the consequence we desire.

When two people confront each other, six ego states are involved. In general, Parent behavior hooks a Child response, although it may evoke a Parent response. Child behavior tends to hook a Parent or Child response, and Adult behavior attracts an Adult response. As we examine our business transactions, we will learn under what conditions these generalizations prove true and what the exceptions are. Transactions can be expressed diagrammatically by pairs of circles marked P (Parent), A (Adult), and C (Child), and by drawing lines between the appropriate circles to stand for behavior. An unbroken line represents overt behavior or spoken words. Broken lines represent nonverbal or covert communication.

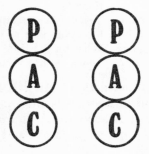

There are three major classes of communication: complementary, crossed, and duplex. The most obvious thing we discover from observing transactions is that when people respond from the ego state implied for them in the opening statement, things go along nicely. Such transactions tend to continue. The transogram for such encounters reveals that communication lines are parallel. We call this communication complementary, and it can take nine forms. Although the following examples deal only with the verbal aspect of communication, they give us an idea of what's happening. If, in addition, we could see behavior clues, the flavor of the communication would be much stronger.

Complementary Transactions
Communication Rule 1. When lines are parallel in a transogram, the transaction is "straight" or complementary. It tends to continue.

1. ADULT-ADULT

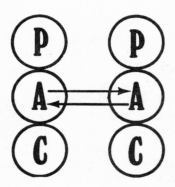

Treasurer:	Should I form a subchapter S Corporation?
Accountant:	Yes, there are important IRS benefits for a company of your size.
Treasurer:	What must I do?
Accountant:	You must file within 30 days.

The simplest straight transaction is Adult to Adult. Often in the form of question and answer, it is the most functional communication because it is accomplished with the least effort. Opinions, suggestions, questions, facts, and feelings can all be handled by the Adult.

2A. PARENT-CHILD
   (Destructive)

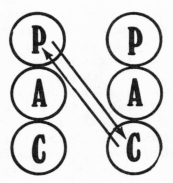

Supervisor:	I told you 20 times to clean that tool crib. If you know what's good for you, you'll clean it before you go home, even if it takes you all night.
Subordinate:	Yes, boss.

This is the old standby where the boss, leader, officer, or some other superior uses his status or power to compel worker compliance. The Parent (supervisor), without consideration for possible extenuating circumstances, demands obedience on his terms from the Child (subordinate). He derogates the worker and reinforces with a threat.

A Wall Street bank prides itself on its "fascist" approach to "check bashing." As yet unable to totally automate the check-handling operation, they engineer humans to be as functional as possible, continually measuring them against preset production goals. Totally realistic about their approach, they recruit people capable of sustained dexterity through long hours of monotonous routines such as key-punching. Borrowing from the automobile industry in Detroit, they use assembly-line techniques to bash their way through mountains of paper. It cannot be denied this in an efficient way to get things done if the firm has an adequate supply of people around with a high tolerance for boredom and it rewards them adequately.

This system is efficient, provided that a worker's diminished self-image doesn't further debilitate him so that he is no longer able to function responsibly in other sectors of society, such as family or political institutions. It works if his resentment at being dehumanized isn't expressed in restraint of production or other anticompany behavior. Those performing such operations feel they're racing against time. They feel that all work that makes people act like machines should be automated as soon as economically feasible. In the meantime these workers get by uneasily by the grace of benevolent dictatorship. Such a system detracts from human OKness and is watering the seeds of its own inefficiency.

The sprouts of these seeds of disaster are already visible. Hannah Arendt in her book *Eichmann in Jerusalem,* and Stanley Milgram in *Obedience to Authority* point to the dreadful consequences of a society based on the Punishing Parent–Compliant Child transaction. They make clear that ordinary people, simply doing their jobs as directed, without anger, can become agents of a terribly destructive force. Eichmann, Arendt pointed out, was not a sadistic monster but an uninspired bureaucrat intent on carrying out his duties much as he had done all his life. He became a scourge by doing things for which he won praise from his mother.

If contemporary organizational strategies denude individuals of their own sense of self-worth (Child) and adequate definition (Parent), and if they strip them of their resources of morality and reason, and replace these with rewards for obedience, all of society becomes prey to demagogues. Using people badly for our relatively indifferent business ends has the unfortunate consequence of making them and everyone else susceptible to the sway of dictators.

2B. PARENT-CHILD (Nurturing)

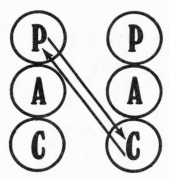

Boss:	Don't you feel well today?
Secretary:	I have a headache because I didn't sleep well last night worrying about my son's asthma.
Boss:	Why don't you take the rest of the day off and go home?

This is the nurturing variation of the Parent-Child transaction. It differs from the Child-Child transaction because of the boss's active sense of responsibility in his approach to his secretary. Although the boss may have some feeling for the secretary, it is not the primary source of motivation. While the healthy Nurturing Parent is probably in short supply in most business organizations, it can lend itself to the abuse of overprotection. Nurturing is counterproductive when it is forced on people at a time when they need to be developing their own strengths. Examples of such counterproductivity can be found in total care institutions such as hospitals, schools, jails, and families.

3. CHILD-PARENT

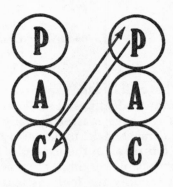

> **Engineer A:** This blueprint baffles me. The draftsman must have escaped from the Funny Farm.
>
> **Engineer B:** Let me straighten you out.

If he is practiced at being helpless and dependent, the perennial Child does not have to look far for people ready to play father and "bail him out." If the Parent figure has a need to appear competent or to be assured of his control, he is an easy mark for the Child. There are times when dependent behavior is appropriate, as when one worker can supply another worker with information that would take a prohibitive amount of time for the worker to learn on his own. That's a good time to ask for help and to follow instructions. There are other times when subordinates should be encouraged to go it alone in order to strengthen their own resources. From the OK manager's point of view, dependency is a very limited tool. A valuable opportunity like this to help another grow should not be missed.

4. CHILD-ADULT

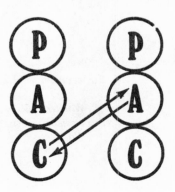

First VP: The boss wants to see me first thing Monday. I hope nothing's wrong.

Second VP: Don't worry, he likes you. This has been a good year. He probably wants to give you a commendation.

We have all had the experience of our Child overwhelming our Adult with feelings of anxiety and inadequacy, even in a situation we have mastered many times before. Berne gave the term "reachback" to behavior that is influenced by an event in the future, as in the example. It is a good idea for the person experiencing reachback to borrow the Adult of a friend to help him identify his feelings and separate them from objective reality.

In the example, the Second VP spots the NOT OK Child which is contaminating the VP's Adult and helps him to resee the situation in proper perspective. The assumption is that there is reality data to support the friend's contention. Although the Adult is potentially the strongest ego state, from time to time it may be impaired by unresolved feelings in the Child. At such a time, an individual may need to borrow another's Adult until his own gets back into the driver's seat.

5. ADULT-CHILD

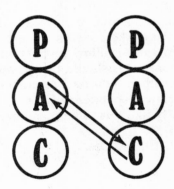

Supervisor: What's happening in the shop? Scrap loss is up 20 percent.

Worker: Boss, you know you can count on me.

Supervisor: I just want the facts.

Worker: We've been friends a long time.

When an Adult request for data is met with evasive, defensive, or merely inappropriate feeling responses, it may take some work before the supervisor finds out the facts. First he has to deal with the frightened or overly friendly Child. With the worker's Child calmed down, the way is opened for the entrance of the worker's Adult. When that happens, both can move forward on the problem.

6. ADULT-PARENT

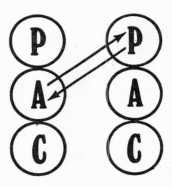

Secretary:	When you're done, will you help me type these letters?
Co-worker:	Your boss has no consideration. He always gives you 15 letters at the very end of the day.
Secretary:	He's been involved with the Atlanta problem all day.
Co-worker:	I don't know how you work all day for a boss like that. I swear, I don't see how you can take it.

Yes, there are people who relate in this way on a regular basis. Because his Adult is faulty, the co-worker is unable to deal with reality issues. With only his Parent to go on, he continually pressurizes a situation. It takes effort on the part of the secretary's Adult to stay on the issue. His lurking Parent is tempted to reply, "How badly you treat me, when I'm only trying to solve the problem." Or his hurt Child strains at the leashes to get even. It's a disconsolate situation.

7. PARENT-ADULT

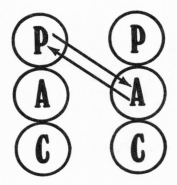

> *Manager:* Please explain to our shipping department that Chicago is in Illinois, not New Jersey.
>
> *Supervisor:* That tank car was mistakenly picked up Wednesday night instead of Thursday.
>
> *Manager:* Those dumb yokels.

This Parent-Adult transaction is difficult to maintain because of pressure on the supervisor to retort from his Parent or Rebellious Child. However, as long as his Adult remains in charge, it can go on.

8. PARENT-PARENT

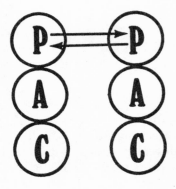

> *VP of sales:* It's his job to sell, sell, sell.
>
> *Sales manager:* A good salesperson gets results.
>
> *VP of sales:* I'm tired of his excuses.
>
> *Sales manager:* Some just don't have what it takes.

Does anyone know what the topic is? Are we talking about something, or passing time playing "Ain't It Awful"?* These people are not lacking for solutions. Their problem is that they can't locate and limit the problem. It's too much work. They'd prefer to parrot answers, even though they don't understand the problem. Give two Parents a problem, and they'll over-solve it every time. With alarums, memos, emergency meetings, and the like, they're sure to leave a greater mess than they started with. Any nearby Adult could be helpful to this situation.

9. CHILD-CHILD

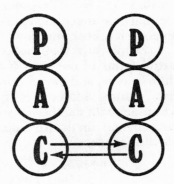

> *Salesman:* How about another round?
> *Client:* Yeah, let's never go back to the office.

Here are two kids at play. They probably forgot what they got together for in the first place. Kids are like that. It's one of the nice things about this world. Our Child side adds warmth, gaiety, spontaneity, and joy to human transactions; without it life would be dull. It is unfortunate that one of the harshest put-downs is the statement "Don't be childish." There probably is no human grouping that wouldn't benefit from more positive Child behavior. It is the most human part of us.

Crossed Transactions

One thing seemingly all managers would agree to is that their organizations are hampered by "poor communication."

---

* Cf. *Games People Play.*

Poor communication usually means that people don't listen, aren't open to influence, and hardly ever say what they mean. "You can't get five people to agree on the time of day, much less the problems confronting the organization and what's to be done about them." The transogram helps us to understand what happens when communication breaks down. Bad or broken communications are crossed or duplex transactions that usually bring things to a stop.

Crossed transactions are easily recognized. We can feel them in our stomachs. When people are being put down or "crossed up," their behavior very likely reflects their confusion, hurt, or anger. Conversational stop signs indicating that someone has been put down include the following:

□ People turn their backs on each other. One of the most hurtful forms of behavior is turning one's back on someone, while heaving and then dropping the shoulders in disgust. The term "cutting" someone is an apt description of this. Refusing to transact with another may be the most destructive "social" thing anyone can do. An unknown poet struck the right note in this little verse:

> Sticks and stones are hard on bones
> Aimed with angry art
> Words can sting like anything
> But silence breaks the heart.

□ Someone abruptly switches the direction of conversation. When a subject becomes too painful or embarrassing and threatens to cause behavior deterioration in a group, someone may attempt to lead the conversation to a safer topic. Everyone must cooperate for this to work.

□ An individual becomes angry or frightened. His body talk may hook anger and fear in others, which may spread throughout the room. Sometimes the tension is so great you can almost touch it.

□ Eye talk demonstrates hurt or anger. People can be hurt in any ego state and express it by glaring at each other. They will feel crossed in their Parent if something they consider to be true or important is denied or demeaned. They can feel crossed in their Adult if rationality is violated. Most often what happens is that people's feelings about themselves are hurt and they feel diminished.

□ You find yourself wondering what's going on. When communication is confused and awkward, it's a good rule to sit quiet and "compute" before entering the discussion. By clarifying and identifying what's going on, we can save ourselves pain and help to get the communication back into productive channels.

□ Your stomach feels uncomfortable, some people are staring at the floor, others are clearing their throats, and others are speaking in pinched or strained voices. This collective discomfort probably indicates that one person has crossed another.

As pointed out earlier, in a transaction the stimulus (opener) originates from one of the three ego states in the initiator and is aimed at one of the three states in the other person. In a crossed transaction this unspoken contract is frustrated in one of three ways. The response is directed at an ego state other than the one from which the stimulus originated; the response originated from an ego state other than the one to which the stimulus was directed; or a combination of the two—both the ego state responded to and the ego state responded from are different from the origin and objective of the stimulus.

Communication breakdown occurs when the respondent does not reply from the ego state implied for him by the speaker. The initiator experiences this frustration of his expectations as a crossing, and he feels put down. Crossed transactions tend to deteriorate and stop. Scrutiny of the transogram shows that 72 crossed transactions are possible. Six are most familiar to us and will be considered here along with the steps that are necessary to reestablish productive communication.

> *Communication Rule 2. When respondent does not reply from ego state implied for him, a crossed transaction occurs. These transactions tend to abort.*

1. ADULT-ADULT
   CHILD-PARENT

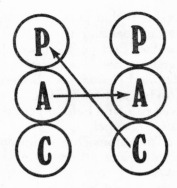

I. *Manager:*   How are you coming on the Polyphonic
                   account?
    Salesperson: (*rebelliously*) You never quit, do you?
                   It's always ride, ride, ride.

II. *Supervisor:* Please pick up on line three.
         Typist: (*angrily*) Why me, why always me?
                   Isn't there anyone else in this depart-
                   ment who can answer the phone?

III. *Sales manager:* Did you receive confirmation on the
                      Gervis order yet?
      Salesperson: (*dejectedly*) I guess I failed again. It's
                      no good. I try like everyone else. They
                      win sometimes, but not me. I always
                      fail.

This transaction causes most of the world's trouble. Here the
adult opening is met with an inappropriate response from the
respondent's Rebellious or Sulking Child. Not in the here-
and-now, and overcome by his own NOT OK feelings, he responds as if he had been Parented. We can expect the initiator
to feel confused and hurt. However, the alert manager will
overlook the hurt Child and continue transacting from his
Adult, going into the substance of the problem. This approach
can be expected to hook the other's Adult and to lead to getting
something concrete done on the problem.

The sensitive manager will recognize the NOT OK
employee who needs support and will seek opportunities to
give it. He will refrain from giving strokes when the conversa-

tion is crossed, since that may only make the NOT OK person feel worse. Later, the manager may offer the employee opportunities to discuss what's hurting his Child. Below are some possible responses to the examples given:

I.   *Manager:*   I can see that you're angry about this matter. Why don't we sit down and work on the problem? It may be that I can help you.

II.   *Supervisor:*   *(after typist is off the phone)* If you feel you have too much responsibility, why don't we set a time to sit down and discuss this? I don't want you feeling upset.

III. *Sales manager:*   Bring me the file on Gervis and ask Chase to join us. I'm sure between the three of us we'll find the answer to this problem.

2. ADULT-ADULT
   PARENT-CHILD

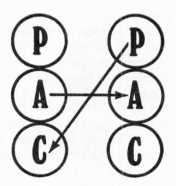

I.   *Worker:*   What time is it?
      Co-worker: *(indignantly)* You too cheap to buy a watch?

II.   *Supervisor:*   Will you please see that this invoice goes out with that shipment on the dock?
      Worker: *(angrily)* Since you became supervisor, you act like you're too good to work.

III.　　　　　VP: Do you think you could come up with a new machine arrangement? I think our present one is too complicated.

　　Subordinate: (irately) Will you never be satisfied? What did they teach you in engineering anyway? We just set the line up six months ago.

We are all familiar with the put-down of a person responding out of a seemingly inexhaustible fund of unkind things stored in his Parent. Such behavior is clearly inappropriate. It is not on the subject, creates bad feelings, increases distance between people, and pollutes the psychological atmosphere. Why, when such behavior is so counterproductive, do we see so many Parent crosses? Here are some of the reasons:

- When we blame or find fault with others, we are unknowingly replaying blaming and fault-finding tapes recorded in our Parent.
- Parenting feels good because that's what parents do and parents are OK. Playing "Ain't It Awful" produces very heady feelings of power.
- There is miserable pleasure in elevating ourselves at another's expense.
- Parenting is more fun and less work than having to get at the facts.
- Parenting discharges bad feelings. Most of us carry around a load of negative feelings about ourselves and others. Since society does not offer us a way to ventilate them, they often are dumped on whoever is nearby.
- Parenting keeps others at a distance and avoids the risk of a relationship.

The hazard in dealing with Parent put-downs is their tendency to hook our NOT OK Child. The solution is to not take them personally. Remember, Parent types are like that without thinking. It's their problem, not ours. Using Adult programming, it is possible to momentarily show a tolerant Adaptive Child in order not to create another cross, and then to return to the subject in our Adult.

Here are possible replies to the examples:

I. *Worker:* (*smilingly*) No, just scatterbrained. I forgot my watch this morning because I was running late.

II. *Supervisor:* (*laughingly*) Unfortunately, becoming supervisor didn't make me smarter. If this invoice doesn't accompany the shipment, we won't be complying with tariff regulations.

III. *VP:* (*openly*) I certainly don't have all the answers. The new alignment isn't working as I thought it might. Let's take it back to the drawing board.

3. CHILD-PARENT
ADULT-ADULT

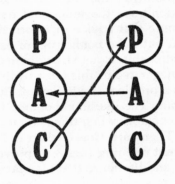

Unfortunately, we often cross and hurt people without realizing it. Many managers have the opinion that feelings are not appropriate to business. Not in touch with their own feelings, they don't understand the feelings of others. They might say, "This is not the time or place for that. Go see your pastor or someone trained in those matters." People who deny the reality and place of feelings cripple their own ability to get the job done.

I. *Worker:* (*dejectedly*) I'm worried about where the whole thing will end. Have I worked three long years on this only to fail?

Co-worker: (*matter-of-factly*) Latest printout shows fractional changes. Better run another test.

II. *Secretary:* (*worriedly*) The radio predicts six inches of snow by three o'clock. I hope we'll be able to get home tonight.

Boss: (*calmly*) You can be sure we will make the right decision when the time comes.

III. *Salesman:* (*resignedly*) We didn't hear from Trayco today. I guess they're not ready to do business with us yet.

Manager: (*dubiously*) If you follow the seven signs of a good salesman, you'll close the sale.

In these transactions, the initiators are seeking sympathy and support from the Nurturing Parent. The respondents overlook or don't see the emotional needs expressed and mistakenly assume that advice or information is expected. Their replies turn out to be nonhelpful or exasperating to the initiator. The relationship is not strengthened and work is stalled. The alert manager avoids this cross by first asking himself if the initiator has a problem in his Parent, Adult, or Child—or some combination. The likelihood of meeting people's real needs goes up appreciably when this is done.

There are times when a Parent-Child reply to a Child-Parent opening seems to prove effective. It is reknowned in life and literature that men facing death or battle are exhorted by respected leaders to take courage and rise above their fears. Facing the French, Henry V charged his men:

> *Then imitate the action of the tiger:*
> *Stiffen the sinews, conjure up the blood,*
> *Disguise fair nature with hard-favor'd rage . . .*
> *Follow your spirit; and upon this charge,*
> *Cry, "God for Harry, England, and Saint George!"*
>
> (*Henry V*, Act III, Scene 1)

When struggling with debilitating feelings each person must judge for himself the usefulness of Parent urgings such as:

Get hold of yourself and behave like an adult.
Stop whining and act your age.
You're no longer a child, forget all that stuff.
In this company we value individuals who can take it.
If you can't stand the heat, get out of the kitchen.

Such statements may prove useful for some; for others, they will only make matters worse. Clearly, a more appropriate response is to show genuine acceptance of the other's feelings and to use one's Adult to get discussion going on the subject.

I. *Co-worker:* I can see you're worried that three years of work will come to nothing. What do you think is the best course from here?

II. *Boss:* You're concerned about getting home tonight before the snow gets too deep. What time do you think we should close the office?

III. *Manager:* It doesn't feel good to lose a sale. Let's sit down and go over the details; maybe we'll come up with something.

4. PARENT-CHILD
ADULT-ADULT

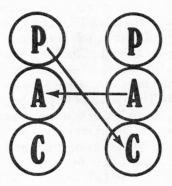

It is an erroneous oversimplification to assume that all business transactions should take place between Adult ego states. There are many times when a Parent request is the most useful and direct way to communicate, and compliance can be expected. For example: "I must have the material here by Wednesday." "We can't have any more mistakes on that mix." "Don't go home until these accounts prove." "The customer always comes first." "It has to be in the mail by Friday."

The authoritative request is most useful under the following circumstances:

□ When time is short. There are occasions, although perhaps not many, when any action is better than none, and there is no time for explanations, clarifications, or discussions.

□ The issue is very unimportant. "Plonking," said Stephen Potter, is "making the utterly obvious stupefyingly clear." Some matters do not need discussion or amplification.

□ The issue is very important. Because of the need for 100 percent accuracy in the pharmaceutical industry, an important strategy is to divide production into small units and check and recheck every step. The hope is to remove operator error by "screwing the process down tight."

□ Others are depending on the performance. The army command to hold the flank at all costs is buttressed by the common sense of self-preservation. Authoritativeness makes great sense in such limited circumstances but does not transfer well to larger issues.

□ The matter is complex and technical. It's far better for an amateur to call a TV technician than to attempt to repair the set himself. Not much good can come out of a do-it-yourself approach. Despite this, the TV technician cannot be expected to be ultimately responsible for matters of our personal concern. In the long run, we are the ones responsible.

□ The decision is problematical and intuitive. Because of their complexity and the absence of hard data, some decisions by experienced managers are probably best made intuitively. When operating "by guess and by gosh," it's probably better to just make a decision and hope.

□ We are talking to an Adaptive Child personality. When working with an individual without an adequate Adult, and when remediation is too costly or time-consuming, our options may be reduced to supporting and Parenting.

□ Organizational norms chiefly support Parent-Child communication. Our attempts at Adult-Adult communication in an authority-obedient system are likely to be met with frustration.

From examining the above list, it becomes clear that there are not very many circumstances under which direct control of another's behavior to accomplish a task is the most effective method. The circumstances that are clear and definite all require a response to actual and imminent danger. In each case, only minimal self-understanding, ability, and responsibility are needed to make the proper decision. For most situations, the motivation, responsibility, and capability of all parties concerned should be brought to bear on the problem.

When a manager who expects compliance gets an Adult response, it is often impertinent in nature:

I. *Supervisor:* (*disgustedly*) I've been after you for three weeks to clean that crib. I want it done before you go home.

Millhand: Good supervisors don't drive people —they lead them by example.

II. *Customer:* (*angrily*) I must have that refrigerator repaired today. It's very important.

Serviceman: All customer's think their problems are the most important in the world.

III. *Banker:* (*adamantly*) I don't care how you do it. I want that account brought into proof before the next audit.

Clerk: That account has been out of proof for three years. I doubt it will change.

We don't know of course whether the expectations of the Parent are valid. However, in these examples it's clear that he has received little encouragement that things are going to get better. Indeed these transactions may only be moving the actors away from the problem.

5. CHILD-PARENT
   CHILD-PARENT

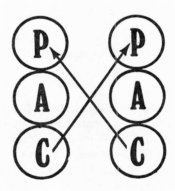

Competitive feelings are in our Child and go way back to struggling with a sibling over who's going to play with the wagon first. We don't have to look very hard in business for examples of individuals committed to outdoing each other. In many teams elbowing and shoving become activities in themselves, quite apart from organizational objectives. Not aware of their ego state, life position, or transactions, some individuals fight for the sake of fighting and assume this is their only alternative. Example I is a variation on the theme "The first liar hasn't got a chance."

I.   *Youngster:*   (*patronizingly*) This line separates the men from the boys. Only a few survive here.

Old-timer: You don't know how easy you got it. During the war we worked ten-hour shifts seven days a week.

II. *Secretary:*   (*excitedly*) Why I've never been so sick in my life. The doctor said I was lucky to recover so quickly.

Co-worker: That reminds me of the time I had diphtheria.

III. *Wife:*   (*flushed*) Our trip to San Juan was the best ever. We spent all day on the beach and all night in the casino.

Friend: (*impishly*) John and I are looking forward to our trip to Rome. He's arranged an audience with the Pope.

IV. *Scientist:*   (*beaming*) I just returned from a conflict lab where they took our clothes and luggage away. Did we ever have a scrap over that!

Other scientist: (*eagerly*) Did I ever tell you what happened at Bethel last summer at our basic training lab?

Because there is a handle in us of fear, greed, shame, or sentimentality, we can be hooked into the perpetual childhood game of "My Wagon Is Better Than Yours." When our Adult is aware of this need, we can unhook from "comparing" and use the opportunity to give strokes to the other guy by encouraging his enjoyment of good things that happen to him.

6. PARENT-CHILD
    PARENT-CHILD

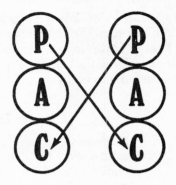

The atmosphere can become corrosive in a team where norms support fighting and medals are given for the biggest put-down of the day: "Wow, You Sure Told Them Off"; "They Don't Put Anything Over on You, George;" and "Wowee, If I'd Been There, I'd've Flipped." Such behavior corrodes group process and makes people sick.

I.	*Treasurer:*	I say headquarters should be in New York. It's the center of everything.
	VP:	(*sarcastically*) Yeah, crime, taxes, and pollution.
II.	*VP of research:*	(*biting*) This is a technological company. Without us, you'd be out of business.
	VP of marketing:	(*sneering*) Don't forget—we pay the bills. Without us, you guys would be back on the bench.
III.	*Manufacturer:*	(*biting*) Too bad engineers don't know anything about manufacturing.
	Engineer:	(*sardonic*) Too bad manufacturers don't know anything about engineering.

When two Parent types find themselves in disagreement, there is little hope for problem-solving. Periodically, they can be seen lobbing verbal shells to keep each other off balance. This can be the opening play in the game of "Uproar" or "Let's You and Him Fight." Each person "hurts" the other a little more. There is a rising effect of louder voices, harsher words, and the game ends when someone exits, slamming the door behind him. We can expect no help from these two. They didn't begin on the subject and are moving further away from it. There's little hope for problem-solving from armed camps. Parent judgments can be exposed by an Adult present who delimits what has been said to what is known to be true.

Ulterior Transactions

Communication Rule 3. A transaction originating in two or more ego states is called ulterior. A hidden message is sent disguised as a socially acceptable communication.

When a manager transacts from two ego states at the same time, we experience two levels of communication simultaneously. A hidden message is sent disguised as a socially acceptable one. Everyone has experienced communication in which both parties understood that they had something in mind other than what they were talking about. At such times there is an unspoken agreement to leave the real subject undeclared. It is common strategy when individuals wish to hide their true thoughts and feelings and present a "nice" appearance.

"No, I'm not angry," he says through clenched teeth.

"That's a good plan, boss," his first remark at the end of a two-hour meeting during which he stared vacantly out the window.

"You are a great addition to the department," the vice president says, unable to hide the skepticism in his voice and the glint in his eye.

"Criticism doesn't bother me," is given the lie by the broken voice, sagging shoulder, and facial tic.

"Now, I don't want to appear overly critical," he says in a way that threatens everyone in the room.

"I got over her a long time ago," he says with eyes tearing.

"You don't frighten me," he bellows.

Not infrequently words and behavior conflict. When this happens, we observe two ego states displayed concurrently. It usually takes place under one of three conditions. First, the individual may not be aware of the boundary lesion when energy from one ego state "slips" through another. Second, he may be aware of it, but unable to stop it. For example, an individual's frustration from the impending failure of a new project may cause anger in him that is difficult to relieve when he perceives that his fortunes may die with the project. Third, he may be aware of the duplicity of his communication and seek the benefits gained therefrom.

In all three cases, when words and behavior conflict, it's a good rule to trust behavior. The alert manager learns to spot the duplex transaction, and if it serves his purpose, he will identify and cause the unspoken to be brought to the surface and dealt with in the open. Occasions where we may wish to mask our true feelings include these:

We feel angry (Child) but want to appear calm (Adult).

We want to appear friendly (Child) while awaiting the opportunity to attack (Punishing Parent).

We are hurting (Child) but wish to appear cheerful (Adult).

We want to appear agreeable (Adult) but are really feeling rebellious (Adaptive Child).

We want to cry (Child) but are unwilling to show weakness (Parent).

We feel friendly (Natural Child) but want to come on as indifferent (Adaptive Child).

We want to disagree (Adult) but an internal voice says, "Don't rock the boat" (Parent) and we are fearful of the rejection such disagreement may engender (Child).

We are disgusted at another's poor performance (Punishing Parent) but want to continue to be supportive (Adult).

It is not as difficult as it might seem to detect others' motivations. With enough behavioral data and close observation we can know a great deal about what's going on inside another person. Behavior training makes us even better detectives. But it can also help us to dissemble better. There are many kinds of situations that demand two-level communication:

□ When organizational norms legislate against certain kinds of behavior that a person wants to express, it's advisable not to be open.

□ When a relationship is tentative and exploratory, it may be best to cool it until the situation becomes clearer.
□ When we want to keep a third party in abeyance. We may decide against leveling with someone in order to bring about or avoid a certain consequence.
□ When we want to express feelings indirectly. It is not hard to find examples where caring or hurting feelings are communicated in a hidden way.

THERE ARE TWO TYPES of ulterior transactions—angular and duplex. Salespeople often conduct angular transactions in which an apparently clear stimulus is devised to hook an unseen ego state. When you resist buying a 36-volume encyclopedia and the salesperson queries: "Don't you want your children to have the best education?" he's angling for your Adaptive Child, hoping his line will pass as an Adult question. In the transograms for angular transactions the unbroken line represents the social level of communication, and the broken line represents the unstated message. There are 18 possible angular transactions where the unspoken message garners a response. There is an equal number of angular transactions where the unspoken message doesn't bring about the desired response. In the examples the respondent's first reply suggests that the angled-for ego state has been hooked. The respondent's second reply is thrown back parallel to the unbroken line. The transograms show only the respondent's first reply.

1. ANGULAR

PARENT-PARENT AND CHILD
CHILD-PARENT

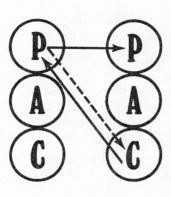

I. *Subordinate:* (*heatedly*) You're right, this must be stopped. I wholeheartedly agree with you. We've let this go on too long.

    Boss: (*fondly*) Good, Smedley. I'm glad we think alike.

    Boss: (*grimly*) Yes, we must set matters right.

II.   *Boss:* (*very angrily*) Let me state once and for all, we will not tolerate such behavior in this organization. It's absolutely unthinkable.

    Subordinate: (*to himself*) Now, he tells me.

    Subordinate: (*tersely*) Now, let's not go off half-cocked.

III.   *Male:* (*unconvincingly*) I can think of absolutely no reason why a man should step out on his wife.

    Female: (*coquettishly*) Between us, maybe we can think of a few.

    Female: (*directly*) I admire your values.

2. ANGULAR

ADULT-ADULT AND CHILD CHILD-ADULT

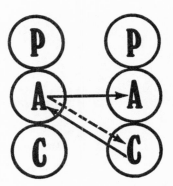

I.   *Salesman:* (*slyly*) This season younger men are buying plaid suits. You may prefer something more suitable to the office.

    Buyer: (*impulsively*) Do you have the plaid one in size 42 long?

    Buyer: (*realistically*) You're right, unusual dress attracts unnecessary attention.

II. Man: (*slyly*) Why don't you come over and see my Mondrian sometime?

Woman: (*mischievously*) I'm partial to any painter who can't stand the color green.

Woman: (*smoothly*) Dutch painters really don't appeal to me.

III. Salesperson: (*craftily*) I'm sure your only concern is to give your children the very best education.

Mother: (*hopefully*) Do you think this encyclopedia will help them get A's?

Mother: (*matter-of-factly*) I'm glad there are libraries to store all those books.

3. ANGULAR

ADULT-ADULT AND PARENT
PARENT-ADULT

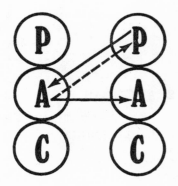

I. Supervisor: (*deceitfully*) Don't like to be the bearer of bad news, but the assembly line has been down for six minutes.

Manager: (*exasperated*) Damn, I'm going to have to straighten those guys out once and for all.

Manager: (*unruffled*) What steps have you taken to correct it?

II. Salesperson: (*slyly*) My worst fears have come true.

Sales manager: (*incensed*) Don't tell me Smithson welshed on that deal?

Sales manager: (*matter-of-factly*) When you knew the Smithson deal was precarious, what steps did you take to save it?

Parent-dominant managers are susceptible to manipulation. The supervisor in Example I knows well the Parent he's talking to. His opening suggests he anticipates an angry overresponse. A chain reaction may be produced among others standing by, with a general rising effect. We expect the problem to be oversolved. In this case, the manager has been set up. As he heads for the line, with fire in his eye, the supervisor stands aside pleased that he has once again escaped responsibility for the problem.

4. ANGULAR

CHILD-CHILD AND ADULT
ADULT-CHILD

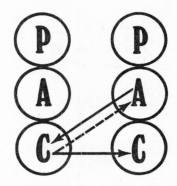

> Boss: (*considerately*) I'm sorry to hear that your marriage has broken up. I know a person of your courage will turn the tables on trouble.
>
> Secretary: (*evenly*) The children and I are doing fine, Mr. Tompkins.
>
> Secretary: (*disconsolately*) Oh, you just can't imagine how awful it is to be left alone with responsibility for everything.

Supporting another person who is hurting without increasing their NOT OK is a sensitive task. Here the boss expresses caring in such a way that it can hook the secretary's Adult. Because the boss is tactful, she experiences his sympathy and is able to respond from her Adult. If on the other hand he hooks the hurting Child, he will need his Adult more than ever to make her feel good.

These examples give you a clue to what "playing the angles" means. The next time you detect someone angling, draw the transogram in your mind, and discover what he's up to.

DUPLEX TRANSACTIONS have two distinct levels of communication—surface and hidden. While only 6 are frequent, mathematically 6,480 are possible. This supports the contention that the transogram can be used to understand anything an individual may think, feel, say, or do. It is a relatively precise model purporting to explain all possible forms of human social behavior.

1. DUPLEX

ADULT-ADULT
CHILD-CHILD

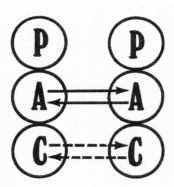

Surface Level

Worker: (*irked*) You upped the rate again last week. Bucking for supervisor?

Co-worker: (*irritated*) I don't like sitting around.

Unspoken Level

Worker: Why aren't you cooperating with the rest of us? How come you think you're better than us?

Co-worker: You're lazy and you have no pride.

It's not uncommon to see individuals discharging bad feelings toward each other under the banner of socially acceptable communication. Such banter hides bad feelings and is a crooked way to give discounts (negative strokes designed to diminish, put down, and hurt another). This is destructive behavior. Rationalizations such as "We always talk this way" are beside the point. People are hurt by discounts. Workers may be victims of a plant culture that fosters "macho" norms. Not taken seriously as humans who want to grow, nor given an opportunity to work out their problems about standards and rates or whatever else may be troubling them, they are left with only verbal attack-defense strategies.

By involving themselves in self-hurting, demotivating behavior, these employees become part of the organizational pathology. Doomed to defending themselves, and denied the joy of working collaboratively, they spend greater amounts of energy in corrosive behavior. Organizing a union in self-defense, they equip themselves to fight better. They are not solving problems. They may be moving ever further away from the real issues. Such "improved" aggression is accompanied by greater pain: it all begins when people become cynical and distrustful of each other and learn to spar rather than to face themselves, others, and the problem. This has an escalating effect. For want of a nail the shoe was lost. For want of a shoe the horse was lost. For want of a horse. . . . Another example of the same kind of transaction is this:

Surface Level

Manager: (beaming) You're a marvel. You've only been here six months, and you've really taken hold and given this place new vitality.

Secretary: (directly) Well, you're easy to work for. You never get angry and you say nice things.

Unspoken Level

Manager: I like you.
Secretary: I like you.

Two people who receive good vibrations from each other agree to limit their transactions to acceptable business behavior. If there are such things as good games, "Cavalier" would have to be one. In "Cavalier," one individual's Adult uses a variety of verbal and behavioral excesses to please the Child of the other. At times the game may even be played for its own rewards.

2. DUPLEX

ADULT-ADULT
PARENT-CHILD

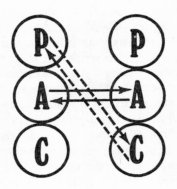

Surface Level

Manager: *(with thinly veiled criticism)* I don't think you've fully grasped what we have in mind for the new plant.

Architect: *(eager to please)* I'm here to meet your needs. These plans are not engraved in stone.

Unspoken Level

Manager: I pay you good money and I could draw better plans myself.

Architect: There's no pleasing some people, even if you walk on water.

The thinly veiled Parent threat is all too familiar in business when individuals are unable or unwilling to surface their true feelings. Notice that they are some distance from the issues. The question is: Can the manager identify what he sees the problem to be? Is he able to identify vague areas of unease and to work with the architect to clarify them? When supposedly adversary situations are converted to collaborative ones, and instead of competing, parties work together to problem-solve, the results can be surprising. Can this manager collaborate, or does he simply want answers?

Behavior training offers a secondary benefit of allowing managers to identify subtle forces within them, to bring them to the surface, and to work on them with co-workers. This improves the quality and speed of decision-making. Paradoxi cally, even though more variables are involved, the rate of decision-making goes up. Hidden communication does influence decision-making. When it is surfaced and dealt with, more powerful solutions can be arrived at. Group integration and motivation are significantly improved.

When hidden communication is not dealt with, people tend to avoid important issues and instead devote time and energy to defending and isolating themselves from what they see as potential trouble. Moreover, when hidden communication is dealt with, the possibility is opened up for wide-angle relationships among workers that can have impressive consequences for motivation, quality, and productivity.

3. DUPLEX

ADULT-ADULT
PARENT-PARENT

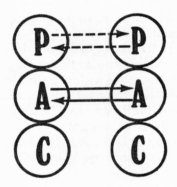

Surface Level

Banker: (*sardonically*) Transfer failures are up 20 percent. That amounts to a great deal of money. Topside is worried, but I told them I have every confidence in you.

Operations chief: (*defensively*) Everyone on the street is struggling with this. The only instant solution is to do away with certificates.

Unspoken Level

Banker: When are you going to get on the stick and solve these problems?

Operations chief: With friends like you, who needs enemies?

How many times have you sat in a room where the anger was so thick you could cut it with a knife and yet everybody kept smiling? The inability to deal directly with anger can really create organizational constipation. Games substitute for authentic relationships. People are diminished, and great amounts of energy are spent on defense and avoidance. None of this activity has anything to do with problems. It is counterproductive to be afraid of anger, to view it as unnatural, and to act as if it were not a reality. Repressed anger sickens individuals, corrodes the problem-solving process, and wrecks relationships. Learning the long and short of the consequences of anger is as important to problem-solving as the cost/benefit ratio. Being able to deal with human anger comfortably puts the manager's Adult in control rather than another individual's Child or Parent, so the anger can be defused and put in service of conflict resolution.

In the above example, the operations chief could bring the unspoken issue to the surface with: "I can see you're angry and frustrated with this problem. Topside, I guess, is shouting down the tube for answers." With the important issues exposed both can stop "passing the buck." This allows their Adults to be brought to bear on the problem by examining real questions: Is there any reason why topside can't be brought in on the resolution side? Who has the greatest resources at hand? Experience proves that those closest to the problem are often the most useful in helping to devise solutions. Need we suppose that all wisdom lies with management? The key to finding the answers is the ability to understand, value, and work comfortably with the Child ego state of all people.

4. DUPLEX

PARENT-PARENT
CHILD-CHILD

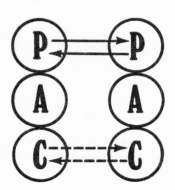

Surface Level

Section manager: (*cynically*) How do you expect me to run this office when you send me the dregs of society?

Personnel staffer: (*tauntingly*) Good managers develop their people and stop wishing for Santa Claus.

Unspoken Level

Section manager: I'm disgusted with these long-haired types and you're one of them.

Personnel staffer: You couldn't manage your way out of a paper bag.

The Parent ego state is an institution founded in the past. It can be used to allow individuals to hide their true feelings under the veil of righteous judgments. One cannot tell if the manager's bad feelings are directed at his subordinates, at the personnel department, or at himself. All three wouldn't be a bad guess. Whether he intends it or not, a manager who spends great amounts of time in his Parent is avoiding his own and others' feelings as well as the facts at hand.

Talking about the relative merits of individuals is not going to help the manager. He needs counseling to help him discover the source of his bad feelings. Once he gets straight with himself and those he works with, he can put energy into solving the problem. If this isn't done, communication will deteriorate further as two Parents escalate their hurting behavior. As in the game of "Uproar," eventually one or both of the individuals will walk away angry. Does each have enough wisdom to recognize and call the game? Is there an Adult around who can help them identify the bad-feeling base of their behavior? If they stay on their present course of exchanging insults, nothing helpful or productive will result.

5. DUPLEX

ADULT-ADULT
CHILD-ADULT

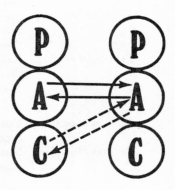

Surface Level

Bill: (*worriedly*) My performance review is tomorrow. What's the best way to handle it?

Sam: (*levelly*) You'll find the boss fair and easy to talk to. It's always a good idea to ask questions on areas you're unclear about. You've had a good year. The boss likes you.

Unspoken Level

Bill: I've got to face the boss, and I'm worried about the outcome.

Sam: You don't have to worry.

All of us have had the experience of feeling "low" or powerless when a hill we've climbed a hundred times before looms ahead as tall as a mountain. Such an obstacle may surprise us because it seems to appear without sufficient cause. Something has happened that triggered a switch inside us, turning on the old NOT OK tapes. We may have developed strategies for turning them off, such as going for a walk, reading a mystery story, and taking a day off—anything that pleases our little kid and turns on the pleasant tapes works.

The best solution is to have a friend who will cheerfully lend you his Adult. Sam senses Bill's disquiet and explains the reality situation and reminds him of his accomplishments during the past year. This is another example of the "reachback" of future events to influence the present. This would have been a direct communication if Bill had said: "My performance review is tomorrow and I'm worried."

6. DUPLEX

ADULT-ADULT
PARENT-ADULT

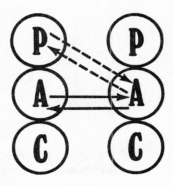

Surface Level

President: (*disbelieving*) Is it true you expect a 28 percent turnover this year at the Syosset plant?

Division head: (*convincingly*) When you consider we've added a second shift, the figures are no higher than last year.

Unspoken Level

President: I don't want to hear bad news.

Division head: Don't worry. I'll protect you.

Here is a somewhat more complex duplex transaction. The president, with an "I don't really want to believe it" tone of voice, signals that he'd rather not hear bad news. "Don't bring me problems" is his attitude. For whatever reason, he'd prefer not to face reality. Here the president vaguely suspects trouble and hopes to fend it off before it gets too close. The division head responds by telling him about the addition of a second shift, which changes the figures and influences the turnover rate. He understands the president's unspoken signal: if there are any problems, solve them; I don't want to hear about them. And the division head tacitly agrees to isolate the president from reality. Not a bad strategy, if you like playing Russian roulette.

7. DUPLEX

CHILD-PARENT
ADULT-ADULT

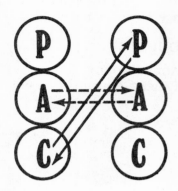

Surface Level

Plant manager: (*anxiously*) The president is coming Friday. What do I do?

Regional head: (*boldly*) When he asks you how things are going, tell him you expect the Kingdom of God no later than Friday before quitting time.

Unspoken Level

Plant manager: The boss is coming. What's the best way to handle it?

Regional head: The president needs to believe his men are omnicompetent. He dislikes problems. He'll believe anything rather than face reality. If you admit a problem, he'll conclude you're weak and ineffective.

In this case a serious message is handled by jest. The serious message is that the president feels it's his duty to make these visits and give pep talks. In addition, it gives him points with the board. He doesn't want to hear about plant problems. He wouldn't know what to do about them. He would become confused and interpret them as a sign of weakness on the manager's part. The president has an underpowered Adult. He will not find it hard to believe the statement: "Everything every day in every way gets better and better." And he'll enjoy making an upbeat report to the board when he returns home.

8. DUPLEX

ADULT-ADULT
CHILD-PARENT

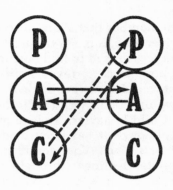

Surface Level

Hungover worker: (*boyishly*) Wow, was I smashed last night.

Co-worker: (*laughing indulgently*) You look like you're in the bag.

Unspoken Level

Hungover worker: Look what a big kid I am.

Co-worker: Drop dead.

Here's one we're all familiar with. Claude Steiner calls it a "gallows transaction" because it accepts and encourages self-destructive behavior. The hungover worker reports on the big party last night, expecting an indulgent Parental laugh of acceptance. His naughty Child looks for a pat on the head. His co-worker goes along with the game. His Adult overlooks the obvious self-destructive quality of such behavior and reinforces it by his indulgent laughter. Clearly it is destructive to allow and encourage another to continue down this slippery path. Each time Hungover's behavior is reinforced, death comes a step closer.

This illustrates the nonreality and negative consequences of such behavior. It underscores the significance of the here-and-now quality of the Adult.

Having analyzed nine complementary, six crossed, four angular, and eight duplex transactions, there should be no verbal transaction that we cannot reduce to its component ego states and analyze for its real meaning. This process is the heart of TA.

Remember that sharp observation of all behavior, preferably over time, is the prerequisite for an accurate diagnosis. You may be surprised to find how much you know about behavior and how much it reveals about an individual's motivation. What would a small child do that corresponds to this particular grown-up's behavior? This is the focus of observation of Parent and Child behavior. Archaic material remains essentially intact although it has been modified, adapted, and reinforced countless times. The identification of rigid patterns and inappropriate feelings through the analysis of transactions strengthens one's Adult. With a strengthened Adult comes the ability to manage one's own behavior and to influence others to achieve the greatest benefit for all.

3

stroking and job satisfaction

WHY DON'T EMPLOYEES have more interest in the company's success? Why don't they have more pride in their work? Why do they only work at 30 percent efficiency? How can I improve productivity? How can I reduce scrap loss, error, absenteeism, and turnover? What can I do to motivate my people? How did we get into this civil war called labor-management relations? Is there no way to substitute cooperation for this internecine conflict?

Is there any manager who hasn't asked himself these questions? The problem is more complex than many advice-giving writers seem to realize. Listed below are some elements of the problem as viewed from a social perspective.

□ Since Parent-Child is the primary transaction of our institutions, we populate society with people lacking a strong sense of personal integrity and of responsibility for others and their group. Social products of our society are more comfortable being either dependent or rebellious. The family, religion, school, military, and business are all authority-obedient systems. In such a society, he prospers most who integrates best. Those who make it to the top shift from dependency to control and may never face the challenges of Adult-Adult relationships.

People who spend all their lives learning to be good followers can be forgiven if they prove unequal to the challenge of interdependence and responsible problem-solving. This is why advocates of industrial democracy often discover that the majority of workers when given responsibility for their work sites look to others for answers. In order to build responsible work teams, companies will have to undo the work of the public schools that taught individuals to be dependent rather than independent.

□ In some ages values are relatively stable and change little over long periods of time. The modern age is not one of these. Values are highly fluid. Society is under stress because of the absence of shared values and the personality traits that make organizational life possible: orderliness, punctuality, accuracy, success-striving, and reliance on rules and procedures.

In the age of alienation we see people who have not fully internalized the social values and normative controls that are necessary for the development of a temperament suitable for continual striving, respect for authority, and legitimately imposed external sanctions. Recently, municipal unions, like crazed animals attacking their own entrails, have been tearing at the fabric of urban society with publicity campaigns calling New York "fear city" and with such riot-stimulating slogans as "We are not going to save the city." Unfortunately it is not uncommon to see once-sound business organizations atrophy and die due to the rebellious intransigence of either labor or management or both.

□ There seems little understanding among some leaders what a relatively precarious undertaking republican society is. As we have seen, great democratic countries like India accept the imposition of dictatorial powers with an eerie quiet. If our daily lives are not interfered with, the majority of us don't seem to care how we are governed. It may be that the issues and responsibilities of a free, technological society demand more than all but a few are willing or able to contribute. The greatness of the American tradition has been that all people contribute to their own governance.

□ "Alienated," "estranged," and "noncommunicating" are the terms most frequently used to describe behavior in our organizations. Impersonality has been carried to the point of absurdity. We are afraid of our softer sides, and suspicious of authentic encounter. Defensiveness best describes the relationship of workers to the company. Scientific management, so called, has reduced work to insignificant tasks, so the laborer enjoys no identification with the company, the finished product, his fellow workers, or the consumer.

Industries' concern for the problem of motivation is of rather recent date. During this country's early decades, scientific management's concern for operator efficiency became the first approach to the problem. "Taylorism"—named after Frederick Taylor—was built around principles derived from the "man as machine" analogy. A person's relationship to the machine was the central issue. Since machines do not have personalities and attitudes, those of the operator were ignored. Aptitude and interest tests were administered to potential employees to identify those most likely to succeed in the company.

"Morale" was the focus of the issue during the World War II era, a time of splendid cooperation, productivity, and integration. In the forties concern for the issue of motivation accelerated as a consequence of the now-famous Hawthorne studies. Elton Mayo and Fritz Roethlisberger's work made it clear that performance on the job was a function of much more than the aptitudes and skills the employee brought from home. Some 20,000 interviews demonstrated that the average employee had a variety of reactions to his job. It was clear to employees themselves that how they felt about the job affected how hard they worked.*

Since the fifties there has been an adjustment of perspective. We know now that it is naive to assume that if a worker is satisfied he must be a productive performer. The relationship

* A number of developments arose subsequent to the Hawthorne studies, as Lyman Porter and Edward Lawler point out in the January–February 1968 issue of *Harvard Business Review*. First, personnel research had arrived and studies were initiated to measure the state of employee morale. Climate analysis studies were constructed in order to know where to concentrate efforts to improve employee satisfaction. Later, more sophisticated research strategies were used to identify the variables that contribute to employee satisfaction or dissatisfaction. Second, training programs for supervisors were established to make them aware of employee feelings and attitudes so they could devise strategies to improve productivity. Finally, personnel people initiated research to demonstrate that when morale is improved, there is a concomitant increase in productivity. This effort, while never conclusive, continues unabated to this day. Although no one seriously questions the hypothesis, the evidence so far adduced has not been conclusive.

between satisfaction and performance is more complex. It is not a question of what constitutes an ideal employee and what we can do to ensure his continued high productivity. Rather, the question is, what happens to an individual when he comes to work? What factors in the total work environment act to increase or decrease motivation? The more valid assumption is satisfaction *flows from and is a consequence of* the job situation. Satisfaction comes from rewards both material and psychological generated by the job.

In general, there have been two approaches to the issue of job satisfaction—the internal-psychological and the external-sociological. Briefly, the internal-psychological approach, as formulated by Maslow, says that we have a gradient of needs that we seek to satisfy—from basic biological needs through safety to social, psychological, and spiritual needs. The external-sociological approach, formulated by Goffman, argues that behavior and its affects are the consequence of and arise from human social arrangements and any attempt to improve satisfaction must have the ability to influence the total system and tune its constituent parts. No matter which approach or combination of the two an individual may espouse, the advice they provide for organizational improvement has shown a remarkable unanimity of acceptance. This advice can be summarized as follows:

1. We must restructure work to make it more interesting, restore challenge and the potential for worker pride through achievement, enlarge or enrich work so it becomes both the reason and opportunity for personal growth. "If people don't grow, the organization can't grow" is a popular dictum. Achievement, recognition, responsibility, and advancement are the tests of the motivation potential for any work site.

2. Supervisors are the important link between the company and the employee. We must institute programs to upgrade their interpersonal and business skills and to reduce their contribution to job dissatisfaction. In these programs supervisors should be encouraged to view workers optimistically and to employ collaborative strategies to assist workers in setting and reaching work goals. No longer acting as Parents, supervisors come to understand employee needs to feel OK, and they create a climate supportive of stroking.

3. We must create organizational vigor by fostering employee participation in the decision-making process. Attempts at industrial democracy were designed to reduce master-menial relationships often characterized by distrust, antagonism, and restraint of production. In their place was sought an open climate of mutuality, trust, and cooperation where organizational and individual goals tended to coalesce.

Transactional analysis has made a major contribution to the study of motivation on both psychological and sociological levels. Its contributions lie in the clarification of the source and consequence of ego state behavior, the origin of bad feelings and their relationship to stroking, and the deleterious effects of games.

Let us look a little further into the description and rationale of strokes. A stroke, as defined by Berne, is a unit of recognition. It may be a nod of welcome, a word of praise, or a linking gesture such as a wink, a pat on the back, or a hug. It may be formal and overt, such as a toast or a salute. It may be silent and not delivered personally, such as a thank-you note. It may be verbal or nonverbal. Positive strokes leave the recipient feeling more alive, with his personal OK-ness confirmed. Negative strokes leave him feeling diminished and defensive.

According to recent research, in a certain European city when friends talk, they may touch each other as many as 100 times per hour, whereas in a midwestern city the rate is only 3 times per hour. We seem to have forgotten that touching is an important part of communicating—it is not the whole thing, but it is more important than most managers tend to realize. It takes many words to communicate what can be said in a brief, friendly touch. Tactile communication speaks to deeper levels in us and is immediately convincing.

Unfortunately, social norms internalized in the Parent make it difficult for us to express direct and meaningful feelings to each other. Obviously this is a harmful and not a useful norm. We generally find it easier to give verbal strokes than to give hugs and friendly pats. However, when organizational norms support discounts (negative strokes) and hurtful banter, the situation is set for employee alienation and demotivation. The put-down may be disregarded as only "shoptalk," but in reality it hurts people—as it was meant to. This in turn gives rise to politics, games, rituals, and defensive pastimes. The aware manager actively seeks to introduce norms and skills of stroking, both verbal and tactile, when it is appropriate. He analyzes the climate of his organization to ensure that people are getting necessary stroke satisfaction for all three ego states. Examples of positive strokes include such comments as:

> Great job on the Excelsior contract.
> You've been helpful in this matter.
> I'm glad we're going to work together.
> I like you.
> Your efforts were an important contribution to our success.

Maintenance stroking is a type of positive stroking that is sometimes called "good manners." Noticed mostly by its absence, it is the formalized and stylized ritual-like greeting: "Hello," "Good to see you," or giving a wave or a handshake.

These remarks or actions "gentle" society and make things easier. Because of their simplicity and lack of depth, they prove important to the receiver mostly when they are absent. If a friend passes without acknowledging us, we tend to feel slighted or hurt, and would seek explanation for this absence of expected courtesy.

Since most people have difficulty feeling good about themselves, some managers feel that the ability to give strokes is like found gold. Helping people feel good about themselves is not only rewarding in itself but has great benefits for organizational integration, motivation, and productivity. As every parent knows, if subordinates don't receive positive strokes, they'll work for negative recognition. Negative strokes or discounts are preferable to no strokes at all. Loneliness and boredom can actually be painful. Because of this, the angriest non-violent behavior we can express toward a friend is to ignore or cease transacting with him. It is aptly termed "cutting him dead" or a "cut." Managers who do not give positive strokes encourage attention-demanding behavior.

Of four bank vice presidents responsible for mortgage applications, one continually presented poorly documented recommendations to the Loan and Discount Committee. Week after week and month after month the other three doggedly did their work-ups to specifications. The delinquent vice president got the most attention and had easiest access to senior managers and committee members. Some even thought that his work was more difficult or that he worked harder than the others—all because of his highly visible, though continually ineffective, efforts.

On the other hand, the remaining three vice presidents received little recognition, precisely because their work was competent. Superiors, preoccupied with poorer production, gave them neither positive nor negative strokes. Things gradually changed until all four presented poorly documented loan applications because "it didn't seem to make any difference." When good behavior isn't rewarded and only inadequate behavior is bawled out, negative behavior is effectively reinforced.

From this proceeds an important motivational principle. The company must actively and visibly reward employees directly in proportion to the quality of job performance. If rewards are vague, unrelated to superior performance, or based on an arbitrary system such as seniority, management sacrifices its most useful motivational stimulus. If undesirable behavior is tolerated or accepted, it is reinforced and stabilized. Undesirable behavior will not be extinguished unless management raises the cost of its continuance to the point where it becomes too expensive to continue.

When performance and satisfaction arising from desired rewards are positively correlated, workers know that the best performers receive the most rewards. Indeed, from this perspective, job satisfaction does not serve to stimulate job performance so much as it indicates how well the company has solved the problem of rewarding employees in proportion to the quality and quantity of their performance. In some places where the incentive principle has been soundly applied, its results have been astonishing. Let us now return to the discussion of strokes.

Negative strokes are designed to diminish, put down, and hurt another. Examples of such destructive behavior include rolling eyes upward, exasperated glances, noisy respiration. Typical business discounts include keeping someone "cooling his heels," tolerating telephone and other interruptions, looking at one's watch, and being overly precise with instructions.

Negative verbal strokes include such remarks as:

You blew it again.
How many times must I tell you?
Not you again?
Won't you ever learn?
I think this job is too big for you.
Have you ever thought of working someplace else?

The third kind of stroke is conditional. It has a hooker in it:

I like you when you're on time.
Good decision for a finance guy.
You did a fine job for a change.
When you're loyal, you can count on me.
You do such a nice job with routine work.

We all need strokes to be healthy and to grow. If we don't receive positive strokes, we'll arrange to manipulate people and the situation—by pastimes, rituals, and games—to get negative strokes. Where managers do not consciously strive to create an open and supportive climate, they force people to fall back on time-wasting efforts that frustrate work quality and achieve only a poor substitute for positive strokes.

In order to understand why strokes are indispensable to an employee's sense of well-being and ability to perform, we must consider again the trauma of the cradle. By reminding ourselves of the origins of our NOT OK feelings, we can give ourselves permission to feel all right about directly giving and receiving OK strokes for all three ego states.

The evidence on the issue is clear. Humans have a profound hunger for recognition and acceptance. Because we did not receive as much warmth and tenderness as we needed from our parents and the society we were raised in, we walk around as half-empty pots. In our infancy, comforting and cuddling accompanied by endearing sounds are of overwhelming importance in the development of affectional responses and a sense of OK-ness. The early years of our lives are the foundation upon which all other years stand. If the foundation is shaky, this will overshadow all succeeding events. It is because we have been deprived of tenderness in our early years that we feel NOT OK about ourselves, expect the worst from life, and cope by means of rackets and games.

This deprivation is not necessarily the result of our parents' inadequacy. For one thing, they internalized social, family, and ethnic norms and fashions unaware of the negative consequences. In the twenties, for example, women responded to fashion's demand for a slim, boyish figure by binding their breasts and denying breastfeeding. Another kind of fashion cautioned against "spoiling the children"—a short-term gain with a long-term loss.

It is also important to understand that the gestation and development period of the human animal is about five years. This is far longer than that of any other species. Most other animals become self-sufficient shortly after birth. Only a human faces his formative years in a radically helpless state. If he's hungry, he can't go for food. If he's cold, he can't seek covering. If he soils himself, he can't get clean. If he's frightened, he can't request cuddling. Before the age of 3 he cannot reason, nor can he manipulate symbols. He can't understand what's happening and make comparisons.

It's hard to understand what goes on in a child's mind when he has only feelings, yet this is a dominant characteristic of our formative years. It is no wonder we concluded we're NOT OK. Moreover, we look out on a world where on the surface everyone else seems OK. As a consequence of this accumulated negative early experience associated with the absence of nurturing, we made a feeling-decision about ourselves that we are NOT OK. We experience this more or less intensely each day, and it is the lens through which we view people and the daily events of our lives.

There is a profound error here. When we were children, that decision made sense, as did the ways we chose to cope with this generalized unease. But today it doesn't make sense because we can understand our victim nature and make a here-and-now decision in favor of ourselves. We can shuck the NOT OK life decision made in our infancy, and with liberated intelligence, accept the OK position. Many have admitted that when they assumed the OK life position, they began really living for the first time. It was the first step in establishing their own autonomy. The OK life position can be empirically validated. It works. It can be proven.

During the early, defenseless years, such nurturing as we experienced came from sucking and touching. These tactile experiences are the primary ways in which the Child receives emotional nourishment. Astonishingly, research has demonstrated that young rhesus monkeys give priority to cuddling over nursing. There is a direct correlation in infants between physical and emotional development and the amount of touching-with-care they receive. This remains true of humans throughout their lives. At every stage, we need physical contact with others to maintain our identity and self-acceptance. As mentioned above, in many places positive verbal stroking has replaced physical stroking. But where verbal stroking has fallen into disuse, we see dysfunctional behavior and its impact on the organization.

When we see people enjoying their work, we know they are receiving and giving OK strokes in all three ego states. Our Parent is stroked when our internalized structure is affirmed by others. While each of us has unique tapes, some common Parent messages that can be satisfied include: work hard, do something worthwhile, carry your part of the load, do an outstanding job, help someone else, support your family, be a solid member of the community.

Our Child tapes contain specific ways of feeling-coping that we developed as youngsters. To discover the kind of strokes a particular individual will respond to, we need to find out what he wanted as a youngster but never got enough of. These things usually give pleasure to the Child ego state: identification with a successful organization, feeling needed, enjoying the company of others, experiencing the excitement of the new and unusual, being admired, doing something on one's own, overcoming difficult odds, being recognized for achievement.

Strokes to our Adult come from seeing something clearly or from demonstrated respect for our ability to collect facts, organize them, establish probabilities, and make successful decisions. From the psychological perspective, an employee's job satisfaction depends on his getting appropriate recognition for each part of his personality.

Admittedly, the distinction between internal-psychological and external-sociological approaches to job satisfaction is somewhat fragile. We can't influence one level of social action without bringing about upstream or downstream changes. If we bring about behavior change in a functioning group, it will significantly influence individual members as well as surrounding systems. All initiators of change must be aware of this phenomenon and deal with it in their planning. There are a number of sociotechnical strategies employed by business today to get at the issues of job satisfaction and productivity. They are management by objectives, team building (Chapter 7), the organizational mirror, job enrichment, and a variety of planning techniques. The one most directly related to the issue of job satisfaction is job enrichment, sometimes called job enlargement. Job enrichment is interesting for the constructs that support it and for the interrelationship of these constructs, as well as for its demonstration of the role of transactional analysis in organizational improvement.

It is important to understand that work itself can be a major source of satisfaction to the individual. Reference is made here to the research of Frederick Herzberg (*Work and the Nature of Man*) and the applications developed by Robert Ford at AT&T. Herzberg defined two separate and distinct sets of factors controlling worker motivation. One deals primarily with environmental considerations. These include company policy and administration, supervision, salary, interpersonal relations, and working conditions. He called these hygiene factors. The second set of factors deals with the task itself. These include achievement, recognition, work itself, responsibility, and advancement. These he called motivating factors.

It is the relationship between these two dimensions that is interesting. The two sets of factors are not related as opposite ends of a continuum. While the hygiene factors by their absence cause job dissatisfaction, their presence has little effect on positive job attitudes. They have the quality of always returning to zero. Both the president and the shipping clerk feel they are underpaid. This is the "Although I enjoyed steak dinner tonight, I will be hungry again at breakfast tomorrow" phenomenon. Hygiene or maintenance factors by their absence lead to job dissatisfaction because of the need to avoid discomfort. However, an ample supply of hygiene factors does not create good job motivation. The opposite of job dissatisfaction is no dissatisfaction, not job satisfaction. That is dependent on another set of variables.

Motivating factors are related not to external matters but to the job itself. It is the experience of accomplishment, awareness of increased competency, and a sense of growth or fulfillment that powers the motivators. All of these are related to the task. Achievement requires a task. The task provides the opportunity for the worker to stretch and grow. The task then is to design work in such a way that people can achieve higher-intensity, longer-lasting motivator strokes. The goal is to enable employees to enjoy a sense of achievement, responsibility, and ownership in their own productivity. This is done by reorganizing work sites to give the employee more control of the process, more accountability for its quality, and, if possible, more contact with the using client.*

Transactional analysis makes two important contributions to job enrichment. First, it clarifies the internal dynamics behind worker behavior as change proceeds, and, second, it supplies the necessary delivery system to implement what otherwise often remains only a good idea in the textbooks. Let us consider first how time structuring and stroking strengthen the job enrichment conceptual apparatus, and second how TA makes possible implementation of job enrichment where its productivity would otherwise be seriously limited.

There is little disagreement anywhere about the usefulness of eliminating, as much as possible, notoriously repetitious operations. Automation is used determinedly to replace repetitive jobs in office and shop. But even after the monotonous operations are gone, there remains a wide range of operations in relation to which a worker's perceptions about himself and his job, not objective reality, are crucial. It is also true that individuals differ widely in their need for achievement, responsibility, and recognition. We can't help wonder whether with the passage of time, even enriched circumstances can continue to motivate. Generals, doctors, and professors get bored too.

Creating human organizations in which people function on a level that meets their deeper needs has to be part of a job enrichment program. It is a basic need in us to be recognized

---

* Neither job rotation nor horizontal loading (expanding the workload) offers fresh opportunities to restore dignity and joy to work. For an interesting disclaimer by the director of training at Chevrolet, consider Thomas Fitzgerald's article in the July–August 1971 issue of *Harvard Business Review* entitled "Why Motivation Theory Doesn't Work."

and accepted by others. We all hunger for strokes. Verbal strokes, which are surrogates for touching, can serve as well. TA theorists have worked out a correlation between how we cope with our basic hunger for strokes and how we spend our time. The six-position time-structuring model identifies how stroke hunger determines the way time is spent.

Time structuring helps us avoid the pain of boredom and loneliness, with their consequent emotional and physical deterioration. The time-structuring model is really a scale of the complexity of relationships, the seriousness of commitment, and the kind of strokes exchanged. In terms of stroking, equal time can be used in very unequal ways. We can withdraw from others, engage in rituals or pastimes, play games, work together, and sometimes experience a moment of authentic encounter (Figure 6).*

1. *Withdrawal.* We can remove ourselves from the encounter with others by withdrawing physically or psychically. While withdrawal can come from any of the three ego states, it is often an Adult decision to leave the field of conflict in order to regroup. Continuing too long under stress may be seriously debilitating. Retreating to take stock of oneself, be alone, relax, and get in touch with oneself can prove to be strengthening. It is for this reason that many companies mandate employee vacations. Withdrawal in the Parent is sometimes based on what we saw our parents do. If a subordinate cannot walk out on a tense situation, he may "tune out." Later he may continue the direction by seeking the narcosis of alcohol. Withdrawal in the Child is likely to occur if in childhood, when faced with pain or stress, we found being alone comforting—we thus trained ourselves to value being solitary or being a loner. Fantasy is the place we visit where violence is unrestrained, pleasure uncensored, and imagination enjoys all manner of impossibilities.

2. *Ritual.* A ritual is a socially programmed use of time where everybody does the same thing. Special interest groups—professional societies, sports car and "ham" enthusiasts, social clubs, fraternities, and political organi-

---

* This model has appeared in a number of writings. Muriel James and Dorothy Jongeward in their book *Born to Win* have a useful discussion that is pictorially illustrated.

	Withdrawal	Rituals	Activities
Definition	Unshared,nontask experience	Socially program-med events where everybody does the same thing Safe stroke ex-change	Common, com-fortable con-venient way to use time in working or get-ting things done – a proce-dure
Behavior	Fantasizing Daydreaming Reading Walking Running Watching movies Playing solitaire Listening to music Sleeping	Greetings and farewells Cocktail parties Military custom Eating at meal-times Customs Bedroom rituals Committee meet-ings Political conven-tions Ceremonies pecu-liar to given group (e.g., religious, educa-tional,fraternal)	Doing dishes Building a house Drawing blueprints Writing a book Mowing the lawn Selling dyestuffs Holding a meeting Attending school Programming a missile
Ego State from which it emerges	All three	Primarily Parent Useful for main-tenance stroking of child	All three

Figure 6. The unequal use of equal time.

zations—structure time in highly ritualistic ways. Many people handle all their transactions as rituals, giving and re-ceiving only maintenance stroking and making no attempts at meaning or intimacy. Life for these people is a cliché.

3. *Activities.* Activities deal with objective reality, usually by means of projects designed to get something done. Gener-ally thought of as work, they accomplish what people want or need to do. They may be productive or creative and therefore satisfying in themselves, or they may be satisfying in that they

Pastimes	Games	Authentic Encounter
Safe, superficial exchanges between people who don't know each other well	Series of moves with a gimmick	Relationship free of games and exploitation
Cocktail party chatting Coffee break talk Park-bench reminiscing Waiting for something to happen	Ain't it Awful Gotcha Let's You and Him Fight Blemish Schlemiel Why Don't You — Yes, But	A shared understanding in the board room A common commitment toward a goal Bonding arising from shared victory or defeat A relationship where weakness is understood
All three	Childhood game: "Mine is better than yours"	Adult in charge allows Natural Child to emerge free to feel and see his own way

lead to studying for doing something well. Activities can be used to keep individuals apart; we can devote ourselves to making money rather than friends. Often when activities come to an end, we may feel lost and useless. However, activities can be the occasion for rituals, games, pastimes, and even authentic encounter.

4. *Pastimes.* Pastimes are straightforward transactions in which we use up each other's time talking about insignificant topics. The weather, taxes, the horses, athletics, and recent declamations of politicians are examples. For people whose capacity for enjoyment is impaired, a social pastime may be

indulged in for its own rewards. It involves safe and polite transactions between people who don't know each other well, without the risk of getting involved at a deeper level.

Pastimes can also be used to explore the possibility of further involvement in games, activities, or intimacy. Waiting for something to happen is the theme of much pastiming; for example, waiting for Santa Claus, warding off bad feelings, avoiding despair, or easing desperation. Cocktail parties are classic pastimes. Stereotypically, men talk about sports, cars, and the market, and women talk about recipes, children, and redecorating the home.

5. *Games.* Rituals and pastimes, all of which are candid, are clearly different from games, with their ulterior quality and painful payoff. Games are designed to bring the initiator a little relief from his NOT OK without making him see things as they are. Since the dynamic of games is ulterior and dishonest, they are the antithesis of intimacy. They are protection for those who cannot bear the lack of stroking of withdrawal, and who find the maintenance stroking of rituals insufficient but cannot risk direct, meaningful encounter.

6. *Authentic encounter* or *intimacy.* Most people have never experienced intimacy. Withdrawal, ritual, pastimes, and games have been their lot. Lacking better information, they have involuntarily accepted these as the natural course of affairs. Most have never gotten into the here-and-now and seen things as they really are.

Intimacy is the direct expression, without reservations, of meaningful ideas and feelings between two transacting individuals. The Adult is in charge and allows the Natural Child his expression. It is not easy. Society frowns on candidness, people know it can lead to abuse, and the Child fears exposure. We have an intrinsic fear of being close, of trusting, and of self-disclosure. Intimacy in business is the bonding that arises between those who have been through a lot together. It may be expressed by the shared glance that reveals mutual understanding, and by the support by another who understands our strengths and weaknesses.

The concept of stroking gives depth to ideas about the necessity of recognition, achievement, responsibility, and work itself. Organizations differ widely in the amount of positive or negative strokes that managers can and do express. The well-trained manager carefully observes the climate of his organization. How genuinely friendly are people toward each other? Do they casually hurt each other with discounts, unaware of the destructive consequences of their behavior? Can they respond to authentic openness and pleas for cooperation? A simple frequency count of strokes versus discounts can give a rough measure of employee integration and satisfaction.

Another way that transactional analysis can contribute to a program designed to improve job satisfaction is by giving employees a common behavioral language they can use to discuss not only the issues related to job enrichment, but, equally important, the process by which organizational change is implemented. Good ideas remain on the wall and organizational improvement programs fail because of the absence of a viable delivery system. A good idea put into a "gamey" organization quickly becomes another piece of company politics.

To ensure that team goals are not frustrated by the unskilled behavior of one or two individuals, team members must be equipped to understand group and individual behavior as well as they do their business problems. In behavior training, managers study transactional analysis from the organizational as well as the interpersonal perspective. With equal ease they learn to handle problem content and group process. Process management goes hand in hand with decision making. They take place concurrently. Members get immediate feedback on the consequence of their behavior, and as a result their learning has a high degree of immediacy and retention is optimized. When managers understand the consequency of their behavior they can begin to manage it to achieve the personal and organizational benefits they desire. Attempts to block, obfuscate, lead astray, control by threat or fear can firmly be resisted by members sharing responsibility for the productivity of their team.

Listed below are reasons behavior training improves the productivity of an organizational improvement program. Seen as goals for a management development program, such training can be expected to improve the integration and effectiveness of any company, division, section, or team. Benefits accruing to individuals include the following:

□ Getting unhooked from the NOT OK past liberates an individual to see life his own way, not as others said he should. "I feel for the first time I am really living and in charge of my own life," one manager commented. Getting free from all those bad feelings and the erroneous assumptions that seem to follow from them enables one, perhaps for the first time, to get into the here-and-now.

□ Putting the personality under the executive of the Adult intelligence reduces counterproductive behavior and enables a manager accustomed to failing to begin winning. Understanding and being able to use one's three behavioral options result in increased personal and professional effectiveness.

□ Energy which was directed toward maintaining the NOT OK life position plus withdrawal, pastimes, and games can now be used for constructive ends. This increase in constructive energy can be used for personal growth and activities which previously seemed beyond reach.

□ The ability to analyze crossed and duplex transactions can lead to behavior change. Almost everyone enjoys an "aha" experience when he understands a part of himself with new clarity. Some behavior takes about nine months to change. Reducing the control of archaic Parent and Child ego states takes considerably longer. In both cases, the theoretical constructs create a solid base from which to start the program of growth toward authenticity and autonomy. The essence of behavioral training is to make clear what is going on in a social exchange and to bring it under rational control.

□ Behavior training gives people a more meaningful and integrated picture of others and new personal insights about their own needs and desires. A manager admitted: "Only recently have I come to understand that I have legitimate needs and desires. Somewhere along the way I learned it was weak or wrong to expect people and organizations to respond to me as a person with needs. TA helped me to understand my legitimate dependencies."

Benefits for the organization include:

□ An understanding of behavior leads to improved process diagnosis. Without such an understanding, problem-solving groups are at the mercy of the most difficult person in the room.

When members share the responsibility for group process, there is a marked improvement in the effectiveness of decision-making.

□ Use of the P-A-C problem-solving model assists individuals to identify opinions and to distinguish them from feelings and from objective evidence. This clarity does much to strengthen the horsepower of decision-making.

□ By realizing that when two individuals are transacting, six persons are actually present, miscommunication can be reduced. When positive stroking is encouraged, when crossed and duplex transactions can be realigned, when the energy put into pastimes and games can be switched into activities and authentic encounter, then the organization is healthy and productive.

□ Managers can strengthen their ability to select the right people for entry and promotion. If a manager needs a creative and innovative member for his team, he shouldn't hire a Parent-dominant individual. If he is concerned about loyalty, integrity, and morality, he should make sure his candidate has a strong Parent. If he needs increased rational horsepower in a technical area, he should avoid someone with a Parent-Child profile.

□ A tense and uptight organization breeds defensive, distrustful, and aggressive behavior. Psychological pollution has a deleterious effect on job satisfaction. Behavior training makes clear the role and necessity of authentic encounter and legitimates caring.

□ A "healthy" person has all three ego states appropriable and authentically functioning. A creative person has a strong Adult and his Natural Child working together. Of the two, the Natural Child is the more important and in our society the hardest to maintain. Vision, a product of the combination of Adult and Natural Child, is a quantity no organization has a sufficient supply of.

As already mentioned, TA is a model of personality, a social theory, and a mode of therapy. Because of its comprehensive nature it allows the establishment of a fully mature management and organization development program. P-A-C is an empirically based model, demonstrated to be effective to improve management planning, organizing, motivating, and controlling. By using it, managers are able to clarify a wide range of individual and organizational problems which heretofore were seen to lie outside the boundaries of management competency. We need no longer accede to the frustration and failure implied in such statements as:

> Old George is just that way, he's always been that way, and there ain't nothin' you can do to change him.
> People are born lazy (sinners, etc.).
> What's the use? You can't fight City Hall.
> Fate is an important thing in life. I guess I was born under an unlucky star.
> I simply can't stand men who sulk.

The know-nothingism implied in these statements is no longer appropriate in those responsible for the health and productivity of large organizations and for a sizable piece of social resource. Shunting these problems to the so-called specialists of the helping professions can at best be only a stop-gap measure. Because individuals, organizations, and society are highly interdependent variables, the definition and alleviation of problems at any level of analysis influence all other levels.

Because of the successful introduction into this country of a foreign product, the head of a domestic company doing $165 million a year in sales and enjoying 85 percent of the market knew the time for tightening up had arrived. Further, his product line was unable in some instances to meet new specifications demanded by a few customers.

Earlier attempts to gain the cooperation of his three product-line operating divisions had been to no avail. Officers met together twice annually, first to hear production goals for the following year and next to hear the reports. Twenty men had direct reporting relationships to the president. Each operating head spoke only to the president about his relationships to other divisions. Since trust was low, playing games was interspersed with malicious belittling of the power, value, and reputation of others. The hiring of a planner and creation of a full department to integrate planning activities aborted. The new planner, either by design or for his own defense, took a strong role in company politics. He was let go and his department disbanded.

In response to a suggestion, a meeting was held for all eight company officers in order to discuss alternative company futures. Initial suspicion abated somewhat when managers found the discussion was open and the president willing to listen to ideas and suggestions. Halfway through the meeting, the comptroller took the agenda and began to make a paper airplane out of it. When it was assembled, he examined its aerodynamic qualities with a critical eye and proceeded to launch his creation into the air, down the opposite end of the board room. No one said a word. Although the paper airplane was visible to all, there was a conspiracy of silence among the participants to see only what the president saw. If it didn't bother the president that his comptroller was making paper airplanes, it wasn't going to bother them either.

This one meeting gives us some clues to three levels of the organizational analysis: the individual behavior of members and their motivation, key interpersonal relationships, and organizational climate and style.

First, there is the intrapersonal level. Was the comptroller aware of his behavior, or was he behaving unaware of his own internal dynamics? Could he distinguish the feelings and opinions he had on the matter? If he was uncomfortable with what was going on in the room, was his trust and openness level sufficient to allow him to express his concerns? If not, why not?

Second is the question of the influence of his behavior on other members in the room and on the whole company during the 15 years he had been with the company. What was the "chemistry" between the comptroller and the president? How did the comptroller impact on the operating heads? What were the consequences for him? Did he care? Did he believe he could change his behavior? Could he explain how? Did some employees like him a lot, and did these all fall into one category? Did some dislike him strongly, or did he come across to others in about the same way? Is he a high- or low-influence person?

Third are the questions of organizational norms, climate,

and style. Is communication only downward? Is information
flow restricted, causing mystery and distrust? Are there in-
groups and outgroups? What is the level of trust? Are people
allowed to be fully human, or is behavior stylized and
politicized? Do members see each other as resources for
problem-solving or combatants to be avoided? Is control data
used for self-guidance and problem-solving or for policing, accompanied by reward and punishment? Are the goals of the
organization clear?

Each of these levels—intrapersonal, interpersonal, and
organizational—is different and proceeds with particular
dynamics. Each has its own structures and functions, laws,
problems, and likely solutions. Identification of the level at
which a problem occurs is an early step in organizational diagnosis. It is, for instance, of little value to solve an organizational
problem of restraint of production by improving individual
behavior. If one member's behavior is self-destructive, helping the boss understand him may or may not help. If the trea-
surer is suspicious of the president's good intentions, helping
the members of the management team to use their time better,
while useful for other reasons, isn't going to ameliorate the
situation.

After the problem level has been identified, the solution
applied must be appropriate at that level. Because these levels
are highly interdependent, a change at one level will be felt at
all others and must be planned for. For each level of system
analysis there are typical problems and therapeutic strategies
(Figure 7).

The threat inherent in all development activities is that
there will be change without transformation. The addition of a
few techniques, accompanied by new policies and practices,
often is but a superficial baptism of the unredeemed. A new
jargon only explains the old way of doing things. Rather than
creating new holds on old problems, releasing vitality, and
giving hope, the new is assimilated into the status quo, and it's
business as usual.

To illustrate, a particularly earthy supervisor with a mule-
skinner's vocabulary was the consternation of management.

Analysis Level	Management Problem Areas	Amelioration Strategies
Intrapersonal	Overenergized Child Decommissioned Parent Low energy — NOT OK feelings Contaminated Adult Unclear motivations Demotivation Adult or Parent dominance	Ego state discrimination Behavior identification Provisional try PAC self-profile Script analysis Relaxation response Strengthening here-and-now
Interpersonal	Game playing Crossed transactions Duplex transactions Destructive fight Impaired communications	Co-counseling Feedback skills Active Adult listening Steps to stop games Improve stroking Assist authentic encounter
Organizational	Restraint of production High turnover; absenteeism Low productivity High scrap loss	Team building Job enrichment Management by objectives Planning skills

Figure 7. System analysis of management problems.

They sent him to "charm school" to smooth some of the edges. They realized not much had taken place when on the first day back he was heard to castigate a subordinate: "Get your lazy ass back to work before I bash you. And how's your mother?" To be effective, change has to take place at all three levels: in company policies and practices, between employees, and inside individuals.

Since companies can't grow if people don't grow, employee training programs today are recognized as a sound investment. Its human resource is a company's best investment. Once limited to job-related knowledge and skills, increasingly programs include concepts and skills related to strengthening intelligence, separating ego states, clarifying motivations, surfacing repressed feelings, behavior change, relaxation response, and script analysis. The country has accepted the challenge of outer space and important strides have been made. Likewise, managers who accept the challenge of inner space find the rewards great.

4

games
business people play

TRANSACTIONAL ANALYSIS has become a movement of sizable proportions. "Game calling" is a subject managers can be heard discussing at lunch. When it is based on the structural elements of personality and their behavioral expression, game theory can provide insight into human motivation and social behavior. It can also be a slick way to aggress when it is not accompanied by empathy and compassion.

The publication of Eric Berne's *Games People Play* in 1964 was a milestone in the behavioral sciences. Adding the dimension of regularity to ulterior transactions and conceptualizing them as games exposed a fresh and useful understanding of human behavior. The names he and his associates coined were memorable because they were apt and disturbing. The concept of games is, as a matter of fact, a relatively precise idea. Games involve people, aims, roles, moves, and outcomes that are predictable. Each individual has his favorites and tends to play them repeatedly. They arise out of and reinforce his or her life position. The words and gestures are nearly always the same. Only time, place, and partners change.

To his superiors the plant head was difficult to understand. Although he was the subject of critical reports and the butt of peer scorn, nothing seemed to influence him. With his crooked smile he seemed impervious to what was being said to him. Always a quiet and nonthreatening person, he stumbled through his career, a tribute to the inevitability of promotion. In order to avoid costly delays and more serious problems in setting up a new plant which he headed, top management assigned an engineer to his staff during the critical construction period. He agreeably accepted his temporary staff engineer and listened to his advice patiently.

A number of serious "glitches" were discovered when the production line was set up. The building was 15 feet shorter on one dimension than was called for by the blueprints. When questioned on the matter, the plant head insisted he had followed the staff engineer's orders to the letter. It was, he argued, the engineer's fault that things had not come out as expected, certainly not his. Oblivious to the frustration of his peers, he successfully executed again the game: "See What You Made Me Do."

The SWYMD player "democratically" accepts advice and assistance from anyone. He then carries out the advice in a way certain to fail. Any mistake he makes can be used against his helpers. When he fails, he feels free to blame them since he was following their advice. The payoff for the plant head was another failure confirming his own NOT OK and giving him an opportunity to unload bad feelings on his helper. All that, plus avoiding the responsibility of the hard work of problem definition and solution. Another example of winning by losing.

By definition, games are a series of complementary ulterior transactions with a snare. What is said and done is not the real action. It is a facade, con, or lie that is exposed by the final payoff or switch. Game moves have a predictable as well as a dramatic quality. When we observe game players, it is often not difficult for us to surmise what the consequences will be. The outcomes of games are not simply interesting or exciting; they usually have a theatrical or melodramatic quality. Games can be distinguished by the tenacity, intensity, and inflexibility of player behavior and by their consequences.

The first degree of a game is socially acceptable and frequently seen. The negative consequences are accepted as normal for the situation. It's the price of admission and membership. Hiring and firing practices as well as expense account behavior are often areas for games.

The nature of the second degree of a game is such that players would rather conceal it from view. However, no irremediable consequences occur if it is revealed. Such damage as may occur is shrugged off as a consequence of dealing with human nature. People may tacitly agree not to bring the incident up. A sizable loss of money because of negligence or bad judgment or barely legal or unethical acts falls into this category. When team members are overly estranged or overly intimate, others may conspire to go along with the game.

The third degree of a game is played for keeps. Player intensity is such it can only end up in the morgue, hospital, or courtroom. The World War II policy of "unconditional surrender" plus the abuse of Hiroshima were examples of third-degree "Gotcha" games. In any degree, games are not fun. Because they are basically dishonest, they wreck relationships and produce misery.

While they could have been learned from parents, most games are played from the Child ego state, in particular the Little Professor. Every child learns, without lessons, how to manipulate people by feigning hurt, pain, fear, or pleasure. The consequence of intuition rather than logical processes, this manipulation seems almost to have a magical quality and may be used as a fetish throughout life. With an active Little Professor an individual can manipulate boss, subordinates, clients, and friends. Most of us have seen a subordinate anticipating the boss's ideas, or a secretary influencing with a quivering lip, or the perpetual jock telling locker room stories. Each is likely to be pulling the same old trick that first worked for him in childhood and that he has used ever since.

Games, as said above, are relatively precise phenomena. Whatever game is played, there are five steps through which players proceed:

1. There is an opening set of moves where the scene is set and those with complementary roles are invited into the game. Remember, games are essentially dishonest. The player pretends one thing while doing another. In the opening stratagem for the game "Uproar," supervisor says to boss, "You won't believe what is going on in shipping." A "See What You Made Me Do" player, looking helpless and hopeless, approaches his work, saying to another: "You know all about this, give me your advice." The "Kick Me" player wears an expression that

says "Please don't hurt the helpless." The gambit of the "Gotcha" player, sounding like sweet reason itself, is: "You know I'm only doing this for your own good. I'm sure you agree if we tolerated such behavior, pretty soon we wouldn't have a company to run." Defeated again, subordinate stands before boss with downcast eyes—openers for a round of "Wooden Leg."

The "Blemish" player, having found a like-minded friend, begins with relish, "Damn place is going to the dogs. . . ." Hurriedly arriving late to a meeting, the "Harried" devotee reads his lines, "Can't get away from that telephone. . . ." The bait is offered. Someone takes the cue, enters the scene and the play is begun. In this last case it may revolve around the burdens of management. It should be clear by now that the game does not deal with reality. We are not going to get into the problem. We're only dancing around it.

2. Of course, the con only works if there is someone around with a weakness or handle it can hook. Fear, greed, irritability, or sentimentality will do fine. The mark welcomes the diversion from NOT OK feelings and responsibility for problems. All game players get a payoff that they value.

3. When the mark is hooked and the game is sufficiently developed, the player pulls a switch or cross-up to collect his payoff. The SWYMD player, having managed to fail while following the helper's advice, switches to Parent and attacks: "See what you made me do. This just proves your incompetence." The "Gotcha" player's sweet reasoning is followed by the switch: "Of course, I must take action." To still his own misgivings he may add gratuitously, "You wouldn't respect me if I didn't." The "Rapo" player, having encouraged dubious behavior, accuses: "I hope you don't think I'm the kind of person that would play along with such a scheme." The "Harried" player collapses with: "I gave it my all, but it just wasn't enough." "Schlemiel," having wrought avoidable havoc, seeks to cover with contrition: "I'm sorry, I'm really sorry."

4. After the gimmick or hoax is exposed, a moment of confusion follows while the mark figures out what happened. Discovering he's been had, anger may follow disbelief. Was it deliberate and consciously devised, or does the player not understand the destructive implications of his behavior? The

mark may switch to another game, or take his leave a sadder and possibly wiser man.

5. After the fraud has been exposed, people collect their feeling payoffs and go home. Often there isn't much else to do. The payoff is the reason the game was played in the first place. For the player it proves once again that you must never lose control, that people can't be trusted, business is a jungle where only the smart survive, and so on. The mark proves once again that he's NOT OK, certain types can't be trusted, he's a born loser, and on and on. It's clear that games are not fun. They hurt and weaken. It is because individuals seek and anticipate their negative consequences that they occur so frequently.

Why is so much time in business spent in games? The answer is probably because managers don't fully understand their dynamics and consequences. Heretofore, they have not felt equipped to discuss individual and group behavior. Moreover games have benefits. Let's examine some of them.

Games help us avoid what we're afraid of, such as failure, rejection, competition, loneliness, or responsibility. Because they are engrossing and the precise outcome is somewhat uncertain, games use up time that might otherwise have to be spent in the strenuous work of self-discovery and problem-solving. They are a kind of narcosis that takes our attention away from the real issues.

Games help pass time without getting us close to people. Societal norms have stressed individualism to the point where people are cynical about the effectiveness of group decisions and have no successful experiences of intimacy. Closeness is perceived as threatening. Proximity causes discomfort and suspicion. It can be avoided if someone will only meet us halfway—in games.

Games are a crooked way to deal with feelings. They help with maintenance stroking and substitute for human encounter. They allow discounting in a socially acceptable way, without the necessity of owning up to our bad feelings and discovering their source and end results. We may falsely assume that because we are frustrated and irritated, the source lies outside us.

"We are here to do business and not discuss behavior scientifically or otherwise," is an uninformed manager's remark that may be a challenge to a behavioral science contention. "That's your problem" means, strictly speaking, that the issue of your frustration lies within you, and the present discussion is nothing more than an opportunity to ventilate your bad feelings. If you disagree on substantive issues, spell them out and we'll deal with them. If you're angry apart from the given situation, "That's your problem." We'll help you understand and cope with that, but let's not confuse the two.

Games help us maintain the depressive NOT OK or the arrogant OK life position. The spiral movement downward of the self-defeating behavior involved in games proceeds on a well-defined course. Starting from a NOT OK life position, the individual looks out to see a NOT OK world peopled with NOT OK individuals. He aggresses against or starts up a game with someone at the office perhaps with the pseudorational statement, "You got what you deserved." The assaulted person responds from hurt and anger, either attacking or avoiding. The returned hurt proves what the individual felt in the first place: "I'm not OK."

The mischief here proceeds from the individual's illogical assumption that what he feels is the same thing as reality. In a not uncommon error that some call "projection," we judge the benignity or malignity of life by our own emotions. But the reality is that however we feel about ourselves and life and whatever descriptive statements can be made about the here-and-now, these things are not necessarily related.

The P-A-C model makes it clear that feelings, opinions, and reason must be distinguished. To the degree that a manager can discriminate among the three within himself and choose those consequences most congenial to himself, he is healthy and functional. To the degree that he cannot distinguish the three and employ the one that is appropriate, he is a victim. People, after all, show their good sense and health when they struggle against abuse and defend against attack. In order to interrupt the spiral downward, we must first be able to understand our own involvement in the process. The Bible is of course right: "A soft answer turns away wrath, but a harsh word stirs up anger."

Games help maintain the status quo when threat appears. They allow the Child, and sometimes the Adult, to keep up appearances, though in a dishonest way. By the use of games, a person who is depressed, hurting, or defeated can function without facing his feelings and can allow those with whom he is transacting to avoid the issue. Willie Loman's entire life was a game based on fanta'sies. Arthur Miller's *Death of a Salesman* portrays that crushing moment when Willie is fired and the whole house of cards comes tumbling down.

Games also allow the low-powered Adult a way out of his struggles. "If they are damn fools enough to pay me this money to run this nuthouse, I'm fool enough to let them," raged the head of a large corporation frustrated by a board of directors that wouldn't let him institute changes he thought were necessary. He took refuge in management games, settling for what was minimally acceptable.

Games are an effective way to close ranks against the new and untried. Change causes discomfort and friction. It demands investment, commitment, and courage. "Who needs it?" the bureaucrat argues. Games are an effective way to control the deviant individual, without the hard, rational work of understanding him or his ideas.

Transactional analysts are determined to eliminate jargon related to the description of personality and its dynamics and to assign common names to the realities. Game titles, which originated with Eric Berne and his associates, have a memorable quality and pinpoint the central mechanism and spirit of the game.

"Uproar" bespeaks the sights and sounds of two very angry Parents moving further and further from the subject. "I Was Only Trying to Help You" whines the ill-humored Child of the manager whose advice has gone wrong and who feels put down. The "Wooden Leg" player, coping from the underdog position, angles for our sympathies as he relates his real or imagined inadequacies. Both are equally useful to the "Wooden Leg" player. "Busy, busy, busy; I'm so busy, busy, busy; I must hurry, hurry, hurry wherever I go," is the theme of "Harried" players. They live in an Alice in Wonderland of blurred images, overstimulation, dissipation, and fatigue. When mind and body finally rebel, they can switch to "Wooden Leg" or begin wondering about their motivation.

Who hasn't felt vexed at the approach of the "Blemish"

player, certain to tell us the latest gossip and bad news in the office. Pushed by NOT OK feelings and a weakened intelligence, "Blemish" players seem able to badmouth anything. It's a kind of miserable support they give themselves. It takes a superhuman effort to resist attacking an accomplished "Kick Me" player who wears a sign around his neck that says "Please don't hurt me."

"Let's You and Him Fight" is sometimes a hiring game. The opening line is some variation of "We like competitors in this company" or "Those who work hard get ahead." In LYAHF a third party causes others to fight for benefits to himself that are not clear to others.

"If It Weren't for Them" ranks among the business classics: "If only we had better management in this company . . ." "If only personnel would send me better people . . ." "If only people would do what I tell them . . ." "If we just had a better sales department. . . ." There is an endless list of ways people righteously push off blame on others. And the Parent behavior of the IWFT player makes matters worse. He can't help until he gets into his Adult and onto the problem.

To be enticed and encouraged into making an investment and then attacked because they were attracted to the swindle is the painful experience of "Rapo" victims. To be set up for a cheap shot is reprehensible. The "Rapo" victim should take time to reflect on his own greed and desire for instant power that made the con possible.

The "See What You Made Me Do" player argues that he did exactly as he was told. He followed your advice and failed, so it's your fault. Very neat. With a world full of people looking to play self-hurting games, the SWYMD player has plenty of opportunity to win by losing.

Because game playing interferes with the business at hand by destroying the self-confidence of individuals and torturing good problem-solving process, the ability to stop games is a necessary part of any organizational and management improvement process. It is also part of emancipating and strengthening the Adult, since game playing is usually unseen by the Adult. How can managers put a stop to game playing?

First, they can learn game signals. Be especially wary of the code words of ulterior transactions. They are an essential game ingredient. In an interview for a new job be suspicious of a comment such as "In this company we are not prima donnas; we get the job done. We don't care if you're friendly and go to church; we're just interested in how hard you work." Go for the Adult in this communication. Search out the content of the message, either by asking questions or by using the summary paraphrase. For example: "I guess you're saying company managers are more concerned about production than people." A direct question would be, "How are decisions made in this company? Is communication only downward? Do you value cooperation?" Since most games are played below the level of consciousness, looking for information can, if done well, be most helpful to everyone.

To stay out of games, get in touch with what you feel when transacting with others. Games can be identified at the feeling level. Look beneath the surface events, do not be misled by them, and identify what's happening at the affect level. Where is the anger, hopelessness, fear, or confusion? Who feels what, and why is it important to him? Learn to identify when people are making you angry. They may be setting you up to kick them. Notice when you are frustrating others. You may be setting them up to kick you. Where does it all seem to be heading? Will you soon feel better or worse? Sometimes when you are strongly caught up in a game, it is very difficult to get out. You may get some help by asking yourself, "Where is this exchange going to end?" and "After the payoff, what next?"

Learn to spot games in process or after the con has been exposed. This, however, must be the shared responsibility of all members of the organization. Individuals armed only with reason are seldom able to interrupt group games and establish open communication. Organizations influence members. Members alone, except in extraordinary circumstances, do not influence organizations. The first step in organizational change is to get top management agreement that the substitution of direct, open communication is every member's responsibility. When someone spots a game, all members join in the analysis of ego states and transactions. Game analysis is a prerequisite to game avoidance, and it strengthens members' ability to engage in direct, open, and meaningful communication.

One of six engineers in an auto plant found himself in a

pointless seven-handed game with his fellow engineers and their boss. The boss was a good engineer but an inexperienced manager. Planning and scheduling were unknown to him. They were always fire-fighting. The boss took the position of the last person he spoke to. The department came under increasing criticism from upside management and downside clients. The atmosphere in the office was tense, confused, and gamey. It was not a pleasant place to work. Finally the engineers convinced their boss to hold a meeting so they could air their gripes and work together toward resolution.

It was at the meeting that the first engineer discovered they were in a game. As each engineer gave his view of the problem, the boss responded: "It's always been this way. That's how it was before I got here, and it'll probably be this way when I'm gone. It's the best we can do. They have the same problems in manufacturing." Regardless of the problem, the answer was always the same. The boss heard his engineers not stating concrete issues but attacking him and his management style. He became defensive and responded with a series of "Yes . . . buts. . . ." He was unable to see that his style debilitated his subordinates. He could not take any blame. That's just the way things were, and they had to be accepted.

The first engineer realized the futility of prolonging the meeting. They were only escalating their frustration with their boss. This engineer leveled with the group about his feelings. "I'm frustrated with what we're doing. Each time we bring up a problem, our boss responds that he's unwilling to do something about it or that he's unable to. All we're doing here is increasing our frustration. Frankly, I don't know why we can't work together to arrive at some new ways to solve these problems. I think the boss wants to improve the effectiveness of his department, and if we work together, I'm sure we can."

The boss could see that they all agreed, and began to see his participation in the stalemate. This was made easier for him when the first engineer shared his own responsibility for the problem. The boss agreed to allow the engineers to make up the agenda for the next meeting, in which all would work toward solving problems. They also agreed that they wanted to improve the work climate and made that part of the agenda too. The first engineer's attempt to stop a seven-handed game was successful because individual members realized that the game was counterproductive for their own concerns. Although stopping the game may not expose the secret motives of each player's Child, it does give each player's Adult a chance to get on to the real problems.

Stop discounting. Any behavior that diminishes another individual sets the scene for ritual and game behavior. It is surprising how much hurting behavior is tolerated in organizations even though it seems perfectly obvious that defensive, upset, fatigued, and gamey employees are liabilities in business. Surfacing the reality and consequences of this behavior frees people to channel their energies into more constructive behavior.

Reward and encourage the giving and receiving of authentic strokes. Positive strokes relieve NOT OK feelings, encourage authentic relationships, and reduce the pressure to play games. Because all people suffer from NOT OK feelings and need positive reinforcement, the ability to give strokes is like found gold. Moreover, people need strokes in all three ego states. When in their Adult, individuals' concern is for their own competence. "I have read your report and thought it comprehensive and balanced in its presentation. It cleared up a number of issues I had on my mind" is an Adult stroke. "I like you" is a Child stroke. "I like who you are" is a Parent stroke. Particularly in technological companies, the early underappreciation of the usefulness of authentic encounter is being reevaluated.

Liberate the intelligence from archaic feelings and external rigidities. This is a difficult task, and an individual needs support and counseling to move it along. It is prerequisite to the interruption of games. The benefits are an improved reality-view, strengthened creative intelligence, and improved motivation.

The definition says that game transactions are complementary and tend to be ongoing. This means they are played in pairs and tend to be repetitive. If you spot a "Gotcha" player, you can look for a "Kick Me" player at the other end of the transaction. The stern controlling Parent will attract around himself a number of NOT OK Complaint Child types. While each receives benefits, they are not, of course, the same kind.

The head of a clinical laboratory assigned a particularly complex project to an assistant who was already mired in unfinished work. The assistant accepted the task and went to work on it. Since he was programmed for failure, the new project soon became another unfinished project. The lab head dropped in repeatedly, pointing out all the possible pitfalls. The assistant made the plea: "Look How Hard I'm Trying," and the impatient lab head finally assigned the project to someone else, saying to the assistant: "I Was Only Trying to Help You."

The lab head has had another opportunity to "zap" the assistant, who has had an opportunity to fail again. Head and assistant need each other. The assistant can avoid dealing with the fact that he never completes a project by having a secret contract with the lab head, who always rescues him and at the same time proves himself OK at someone else's expense. The most obvious Adult questions escape them both: Why assign a task to a person who is already overworked? Why is the assistant unable to finish a project satisfactorily? Both use the nonreality of their complementary games to maintain their own life positions. They may go through their entire lives living these fictions.

The rest of this chapter is devoted to transogram analysis of some of the more common business games. The central dynamics of each is explicated in the paragraph that analyzes what is really going on at the unspoken level.

GOTCHA

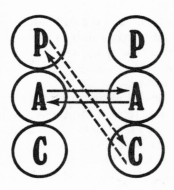

Surface Level

Boss: (*snidely, to a late employee hurrying to his desk*) What time is it?

Subordinate: I'm afraid I'm late again.

Boss: (*angrily*) That's the third time this month. You force me to take action. If I didn't, you understand everyone in the plant would soon feel free to be late. We can't run a business like that.

Unspoken Level

Boss catches subordinate in a bungle or goof and feels free to punish because the subordinate "has it coming." The boss punishes all out of proportion to the offense and feels righteous about it at the same time because "He only got what he deserved." It's a trapping game used as a substitute for facing the problem. The payoff is the crooked unloading of bad feelings.

KICK ME

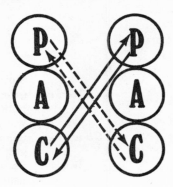

Surface Level

Worker: (*dejectedly*) It looks like I messed up again.

Supervisor: (*angrily*) That's the third time this month.

Worker: (*rebelliously*) You're not so smart either.

Supervisor: (*finally*) Turn in your time. You've got your walking papers.

Unspoken Level

Worker's body language, called a "sweatshirt message," says, "Please don't hurt the helpless." If this does not provoke attack, the worker will exhibit increasingly provocative behavior until others oblige, out of exasperation. The payoff is that the player, having arranged to fail again, shifts to "Why Does This Always Happen to Me?"

AIN'T IT AWFUL

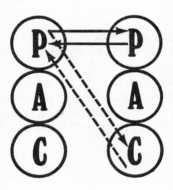

Surface Level

Worker: (*provocatively*) Have you seen the new policy on vacations? They know I always take August off.

Co-worker: (*going along*) It's no wonder unions are getting stronger.

Worker: Speaking of unions, did you hear . . . ?

Unspoken Level

First-degree "Ain't It Awful" games are mildly pleasant. A variation is "Look What They're Doing to Us Now." While the player is overtly distressed, he is covertly pleased with the satisfactions he can wring from his misfortunes. Payoff: a sense of OK arising from the pleasure of blaming the ubiquitous "they," plus the avoidance of the responsibility and hard work of thinking clearly.

BLEMISH

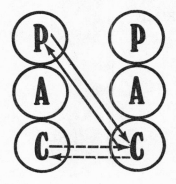

Surface Level

VP: (*irately*) Quality control has been letting too much get past them. If you don't stay on top of them they're sure to get lax.

Supervisor: (*assenting*) We'll have to tighten up and get rid of the bad apples.

VP: Can't you do something to keep them awake? They hang around the tool crib too much and their coveralls are dirty. And another thing. . . .

Unspoken Level

For the "Blemish" player, there is nothing he can't find fault with. By casting blame, he hopes others won't recognize his helplessness and incompetence. Prying and snooping behavior are characteristic of the "Blemish" player. He is the source of bickering and petty dissension in everyday life. When the NOT OK Child comes on Parent, he hopes to hide his inadequate intelligence while discharging bad feelings. The payoff for him is negative reassurance while he staves off depression from self-doubts. Understanding the source of his NOT OK feelings and using his Adult to stop discounting is the remedy for the "Blemish" player. It is difficult to understand that when blaming others, we most often are talking about ourselves.

UPROAR

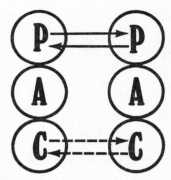

Surface Level

VP of sales: (*despairingly*) I'm told your bid was late again.

Sales manager: (*defensively*) Manufacturing never gets their costing reports done on time.

VP of sales: Excuses don't get orders.

Sales manager: I'm no magician. Why don't you ask manufacturing—they're already six months behind on orders for the new series.

Unspoken Level

The game starts with a discount as both players avoid the hard work of arriving at clear definitions, open communication, and adequate causation. People can shout answers a long time without ever moving closer to the problem. In addition, as ill feelings arise and communication becomes increasingly anti-personal, the discussion rapidly deteriorates to the level of "So's your old man."

The trouble with a destructive fight is that it must all be undone before parties to the transaction can return to problem-solving. Bad feelings will have to be mended, misconceptions corrected, and trust reestablished before they can return to the issues confronting them. Smoothing-over counsel such as "Let's all act civil; I'm sure nothing personal was meant by that exchange" hardly ever works. It overlooks the fact that individuals are hurting or smirking. As long as their Child remains hooked, they have little Adult resource to deal with here-and-now issues.

By discussing the behavioral breakdown, using the transogram and rules of communication, relationships can be re-established. More important, individuals are better able to avoid breakdowns in the future. One should always be wary of put-downs and look beneath them for the bad feelings that are their source. The payoff for "Uproar" is the avoidance of authentic encounter and the discharge of bad feelings.

WOODEN LEG

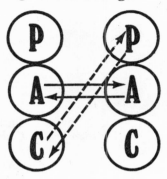

Surface Level

Boss: (*evenly*) You omitted an important consideration in this report. Please tighten it up.

Subordinate: (*pleading*) I hope you're not expecting too much of me. Remember, I never finished college like you. You shouldn't measure others by yourself.

Unspoken Level

The "Wooden Leg" player assumes the role of victim. Some people *are* victims; others assume the role for its benefits. Coping from the victim role, the "Wooden Leg" player exploits the value of a real or imagined handicap. It's another version of how to win by losing. By calling on the boss's humanity and sense of fair play for the weak, the "Wooden Leg" player may not only get strokes but also escape responsibility for his behavior. The weak control the strong when feelings are evoked instead of reality-based decisions. The pheasant that fakes a broken wing or the antelope that fakes a broken leg does so to draw attention away from the real issue—the presence of its young. The "Wooden Leg" player seeks the same distraction—from the issues of his work.

IF IT WEREN'T FOR THEM

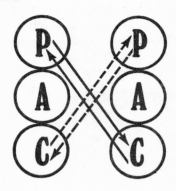

Surface Level

Division head: (*judgmentally*) If it weren't for the conservative ideas of top management, my division, I am sure, could be twice as profitable.

Comptroller (*acquiescent*) You're right. We need new pricing policies, better internal auditing, and we could use newer equipment.

Unspoken Level

This is another victim game, subtitled "Looking for a Savior." Rather than thinking into the problem, the victim casts blame on others, above or below. In so doing, he avoids the work of using his own Adult to solve problems. He hopes this will pass unnoticed among his complaints. The payoff is that he is saved again from facing the problem. Interrupting the IWFT player, as in all games, involves getting him to focus on reality in the here-and-now. What are pros and cons of management's position? Is it true that topside behaves only in political ways? Is it clear that they wouldn't respond to a better idea if they heard one?

SEE WHAT YOU
MADE ME DO

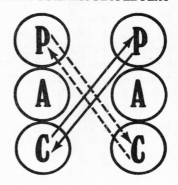

Surface Level

Manager: (*imploringly*) What do I do now? Blacks won't work with whites. Supervisors are lying down on the job. The union is threatening to strike.

Personnel officer: (*supportively*) Why don't you call the department together and see what their beefs are? Ask them to handle grievances as agreed upon. Read the contract to them and insist on compliance.

Manager: (*later*) I did what you said, and there was a brawl. Your advice only made matters worse.

Unspoken Level

The SWYMD player can fail in the best of circumstances. Seeming reasonable and open to advice, he asks for help from assistants. Any mistake he makes can be used against them— they soon learn, to their chagrin and sorrow. When he fails, he feels free to blame them, since he was following their advice. And he will fail. This is another non–reality-based game that is incomprehensible without an understanding of an individual's profound sense of NOT OK and his desire not to change things, face reality, and grow up. It's a self-hurting game he plays, whereby failing again confirms his NOT OK feelings. At the same time he turns the tables on those supposedly stronger helpers who were giving him advice. He shifts to the persecutor role and punishes—"It's all your fault." Some people are persecutors; others merely act the role from time to time for the benefits they obtain.

The irony of a game of SWYMD is that much of the conversation seems to be about business problems. Sometimes it's only after the switch that the painful truth is realized. Beware of duplex transactions, and test to see if your communications are being accurately decoded.

I WAS ONLY TRYING TO HELP YOU

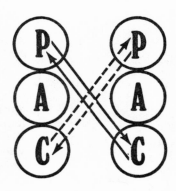

Surface Level

Supervisor: (*patronizingly*) If you do exactly what I tell you, it will work out fine.

Worker: (*later*) I did as you said, but for some reason it doesn't work.

Supervisor: You must have done something wrong. Now let me explain it carefully again.

Worker: (*still later*) I've wasted all day on this and it's still not right. You don't know what you're talking about.

Supervisor: (*defensively*) I was only trying to help you.

Unspoken Level

The IWTHY player arranges to give help that causes failure. Controlled by cynicism and a sense of NOT OK, he is not sufficiently in reality to fully understand the problem, the worker, or himself. His ulterior motive, of which he is, doubtless, unaware, is to prove that people are disappointing and ungrateful. He gives help that fails and then feels self-righteously offended in the failure because "Nobody does what I tell them." When accosted by the angry helpee, he laments: "I was only trying to help you." In addition to reinforcing his NOT OK feelings, he never has to face the unfamiliar rigors of success.

There is an almost universal drive within people to maintain the relative comfort of the status quo and to flee the discomfort of change. In many cases they never change this lifelong pattern and break through their defenses and rationalizations to new possibilities for growth insight and taking on new challenges.

HARRIED

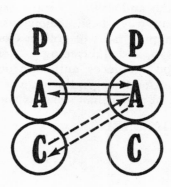

Surface Level

Manager: (hurriedly) We've got to get this report on the boss's desk today. I'm late already for the 9 A.M. meeting and have three client appointments this afternoon. After dinner with a customer, I'm taking the night plane to Dallas.

Secretary: What do you want to do about those calls on your desk?

Manager: I'll get to them next week. I'll dictate now if you're ready.

Unspoken Level

Willing to do anything to avoid coming to terms with and understanding his own consciousness, the "Harried" player drives himself until mind and body rebel and lapse into exhaustion. While sick, he expects approval for his "soldiering" and at the same time gathers strokes due the wounded. In the typical "Harried" player, cumulative fatigue and sickness combine and he ceases to function. Sometimes the psychic shock of sickness ejects him into reality, causing him to reassess his behavior. This may lead to replacing "workaholic" compulsiveness with more aware behavior. Most, unfortunately, will only transfer their energies to the game "Wooden Leg" or "See What You Made Me Do."

A milder version of "Harried" is played by those who for more or less convincing reasons travel about the world, holding meetings, making studies, conducting on-site inspections, or attending conferences. With almost unlimited expense accounts and ability to find reasons for doing what they want to do anyway, these aficionados of the good life can be heard swapping tales of golf in Geneva, the sights and sounds of Tokyo, and sightseeing in Rome. "Get While the Getting Is Good" replaces authentic consciousness and reality-based considerations. In this case cynicism and *Weltschmerz* are the payoff rather than sickness and fatigue.

SCHLEMIEL

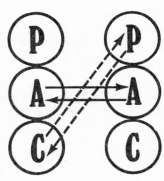

Surface Level

Draftsman: (*apologetically*) Oops, I spilled the ink.

Architect: Damn, two days' work shot.

Draftsman: I'm sorry, I guess I'm just clumsy.

Architect: Forget it. You didn't mean to do it. It was an accident. I'll clean it up.

Unspoken Level

People tend to play their games over and over. They seek opportunities to do the untoward, such as spill something on someone, burn a fabric, get actively ill, or create a scene. We conclude that these social hoaxes are intended because they occur repeatedly. These people enjoy the havoc they create and seek at the same time to escape the just consequences of their gaffe. By appearing contrite, the player makes the victim

feel he must forgive what appears to be accidental. Politeness
must be met with politeness. You have to forgive things that
appear accidental. The "Schlemiel" player focuses attention
on himself, hurts others, and at the same time receives strokes
for being socially polite. This is another example of coping
from the underdog position.

WHY DON'T YOU— YES, BUT

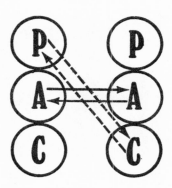

Surface Level

Steward: And that's my problem. Any suggestions?

Supervisor: Have you tried . . . ?

Steward: Yes, I tried that last time and it didn't
work.

Supervisor: Well, why don't you . . . ?

Steward: That won't work because. . . .

Supervisor: (*desperately*) Well, then, I guess you'll
have to. . . .

Steward: Yes, but I tried that too.

Unspoken Level

The name given this old chestnut by Berne and his associates
accurately pinpoints its central dynamic. Some people ask for
help only to use the occasion to put the helper down. "Why
Don't You—Yes, But" (YDYB) might be alternately titled: "See
If You Can Find a Solution I Can't Find Fault With." By rejecting all suggestions, the YDYB player proves himself better than
the helper. Because of the supposed nobility of helping, few
people can resist the invitation to assist. Most individuals, after
they have volunteered their services and been put down, get
the message. Some never do. The YDYB player gets the neces-

sary supportive strokes of friendly advice, and when the switch comes, he also has the pleasure of rejecting each proffered solution and, thereby, showing the superiority of his own experience and insight.

LET'S YOU AND HIM FIGHT

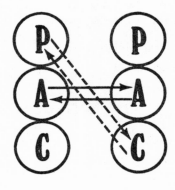

	Surface Level
College recruiter:	(*calculatingly*) We are all great competitors in this company. The marketplace is an indifferent world where the fittest survive. We work hard, spend long hours, and ask no quarter. Cream always rises to the top. Keep your eye on the target and you'll get ahead. If you make it in this company, you can hold up your head anywhere.
New MBA:	My daddy always said, "If you can't stand the heat, get out of the kitchen."

Unspoken Level

Socializing the young is one way that culture perpetuates itself. The con occurs when company norms support competition whether it is appropriate to the situation or not. Players are maneuvered into fighting, with the implication that the decision will prove who is the best and who will receive promotions and other rewards. In reality it may demonstrate only which person is the most gullible. The boss who caused the fight merely switches the game if he doesn't like the consequences. He may, for example, go with a third party "to get a new slant on things." The payoff to the player (the recruiter) is that he weeds people out with the unspoken philosophy that honest competition is for suckers who can't spot the boss's games and get into the big time.

GEE, YOU'RE WONDERFUL, PROFESSOR

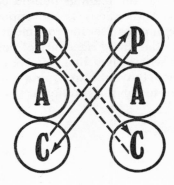

Surface Level

Vice president: Things have certainly gotten better around here since you arrived. I don't know where we'd be today if you hadn't joined us. We need more people like yourself around.

President: (*to himself*) You're uncommonly perceptive.

Unspoken Level

This game might be called "Flattery Will Get You Almost Anywhere." The GYWP player has designs on the helper or boss. Once he has beguiled him, he can use him or make him look foolish and move on to another mark. There is a good deal of the Little Professor in the GYWP player. Flattery has almost a magical quality over some individuals. The GYWP player maintains his life position while adding another scalp to his belt.

Duplicity is the basis of all games. And games, as Berne made clear, are not fun. They cause misery. When a person's behavior is observably different from his stated motivation, beware of being invited into a game. We term a person "unconscious" who is neither aware of the consequences of his behavior nor in touch with its true motivation. If he attempts to assign a reason for his behavior other than can be supported by the facts, we call this spurious reason a "rationalization."

The sure way to avoid game playing is to identify within ourselves the feelings behind our behavior and "own up" to them. Authenticity is the opposite of game playing. Teams show impressive improvement when they move out from under the dread necessity of politics and games and begin to "talk where they live." It is no wonder—all the energy that previously went into coping with bad process can now be directed to solving problems.

5

the transactional analysis of listening

THE HIGHER a manager rises in a company, the more his success is dependent on the efforts of others, and the less he is able to rely on his own direct actions. The amount of listening an individual does is directly proportional to his rank on the pyramid. Listening behavior and attitudes in business transactions contribute significantly, if not decisively, to how individuals view each other.

The breaking down of speaking-listening transactions into their component ego states reveals that there is more going on in listening than meets the eye. To continue the metaphor, we can hear more accurately and understand something about the speaker's motivations if our critical eye is tuned to his behavior. People facing each other may or may not be talking to each other. They may or may not have ulterior motives. People transacting may or may not be listening to each other.

The operations head of an oil refinery had a reputation of being a man of few words. Week after week he would sit quietly through six-hour "position" meetings in the plant manager's office on Monday mornings. He responded to direct questions and made his production report when his turn came.

His listening behavior was interesting. For relatively long periods of time he would stare out the window or look blankly around the room. At other times he would take out file cards he always carried with him and make copious notes. At still other times he would sit with his arms folded and stare stonily at the center of the table or over the speaker's head. Without saying a word, he conveyed what he was thinking to others on the team. His indifference was manifested by his Child taking flight into pleasurable fantasies as he stared wistfully out the window. When an idea came to him, he wrote it down. When he got back to the office, he got on the phone and discussed the idea, often with someone who had been at the meeting. When he disagreed with what was being said, he showed disapproval by frowning and staring.

All this came from a man reknowned for his few words. He didn't need them. He controlled people by what he didn't say. Although they could have responded to verbal judgments from him, they didn't know how to handle his nonverbal communication. Without saying much, he was a high-influence member of the team, escaping the rigors of clear verbal communication by controlling others only with his behavior. While speaking, everyone was afraid of his angry frowns and stares. They "eye-checked" with him repeatedly. Angry "eye-talk" accompanied by sighing says either "I disapprove of your position" or "I dislike you." Nonverbal communication cannot cogently disagree with substantive matters on the table. It can only confuse and hurt individuals.

For the rest of the members on this team, the way out of this trap was to make the operations head's behavior, or "process" as we have called it, part of the discussion. Making him "own up" to his behavior and explain his position clarified discussions, improved team climate, and denied him cheap victories.

Franklin Ernst makes the following three-part distinction in *Who's Listening?* Behavior of the not-now-talking person can be divided into: withdrawal, scanning, and listening. Withdrawal is avoidance of contact with the speaker. It is evidenced by the cessation of voluntary muscle activity as the body becomes lethargic. The interval between eye blinks expands beyond four to six seconds. When these signs are present, we can conclude that the individual has effectively ceased to listen. Withdrawal is highly debilitating to the talking-listening of others. A turned-off person can cause high levels of discomfort in a social situation. Such a person is often experienced as threatening. Because of its negative effect on others, turning off is frequently used as a form of hostility. Being overlooked or ignored can be a very unsettling experience and, as we witnessed with the operations head, can also be a method of persuasion.

Scanning is distinguished from listening. It is the preconscious auditory surveying of the social environment for suitable stimuli to respond to. Although perhaps unaware of the process, all of us have sat through meetings semi-alert only to things we want or need to hear. We pick up and listen to things just long enough to ascertain their probable usefulness to us. Like radar, signals appear as tiny blips on the screen of our consciousness, held there for possible focusing and attention for a short interval following the event. Functioning just at the level of awareness, we hear what we need or wish to hear and ignore the rest.

If stronger or more important stimuli which make the matter immediately relevant to us are not received, what appears on the screen is soon discarded. If such stimuli are received, the matter is brought forward to the conscious attention to be dealt with. "How do you feel about this, Smith?" will likely cause Smith to stop scanning and start thinking. If the communication has no attention grabber in it, the auditory image will decay over the succeeding 60 seconds and the individual will return to scanning.

Listening is an activity which may take place from any ego state. Behavior of the not-now-talking person reveals which ego state is activated. When there is no movement, we conclude that there is no listening. Systematic observation demonstrates what common sense reports: listening behavior influences the person speaking. Such behavior includes movements and nonmovements, gestures and mannerisms, production of vocal and nonvocal sounds, alterations of body posture—in short, all those things which taken together reveal the operant ego state. Listening is a much more active behavior than most people realize. To be listening means to be alert, stimulated, involved, captured, attentive, open. Brainwave tracings show a different pattern when a person is listening as compared to when he is scanning or when his brain is in neutral (withdrawal).

We define listening as the way an individual behaves in

response to or as a stimulus for the audible environment. It is the focusing, converging, associating, and selecting done for the spoken words and for the behaviors of the speaker. The active listener blinks his eyes no fewer than once every three or four seconds. With this basic information a manager can estimate with a high degree of confidence which individuals are or are not listening to whoever is speaking. Listening, as with all behavior, is associated with the three ego states. The Parent's opinions and rigidities, the Child's fixated and archaic feelings, the Adult's cool calculations—each state is associated with characteristic external behavior related to listening.

Adult listening is manifested by an attentive attitude accompanied by considerable motion. The head is squared with the vertical and horizontal plane. A variety of vocal sounds may confirm and encourage the speaker. Good Adult listening has the ability to improve the speaker's thinking. Adult strokes stimulate the mind and encourage the doubting spirit. The following are dialogue devices associated with Adult listening:

□ Summary paraphrase restates speaker's position in terse form, usually beginning with "What I understand you to say is that. . . ."
□ Open questions invite further clarification, exploration of tangential issues, or presentation of further data or arguments.
□ Supporting statements supplied by Adult listener reinforce speaker's position from a new direction or with other evidence not adduced by speaker.
□ Empathetic statements support speaker as a human being and applaud his efforts. This is not the same thing as agreeing with his position.

The single most significant Adult listening behavior is the head vertical with eyes parallel to the horizon. This portrays a level-headed, straightforward consideration of the situation at hand. It is evidenced by the gaze periodically shifting from location to location and by intermittent changing of the position of the trunk and limbs. It can be observed that when the listener's Adult is in charge, from time to time there will be a tilting of the head as the listener checks his other ego states, for example, with the question "How does my Child feel about this?" Usually the listener's head will return to a level position within 30 seconds.

Adult responses to questions characteristically follow a four-second lag during which the speaker can be seen "computing" his answer. When an individual responds to a question in less than four seconds, he's probably replaying pre-programmed material (tapes), instead of computing with here-and-now data. Adult responses have a deliberate on-target quality.

Listening from our Child ego state manifests the way we listened when we were children. There are five stop-action portraits that answer the question "What is the little child doing in that grown-up body?"

1. The itchy kid is impatient and restless, listening like a 5-year-old during religious services. Short attention span with gross body movements toward and away from speaker are characteristic as the individual shifts between Complaint and Rebellious Child. Impulsively he may blurt out a new discovery or be overwhelmed by a new idea. Contrary to opinions of preachers, teachers, and parents, a lot of listening can be going on.

2. The embarrassed child listens, with rising facial color and "Aw, shucks" demeanor when caught in a bungle. Related to this is the coy child listening with head down, turned at a slight angle away from speaker, briefly glancing upward out of the corner of the eye with a "You wouldn't hurt poor helpless little ol' me, would you?" invitation.

3. The pouting child with projected lower lip reveals his inner rebelliousness. Open rebellion is portrayed by firm jaw, lips pursed, stony-faced squint, foot stamping, and "No, I won't, and you can't ever make me" tacitly or overtly expressed.

4. The pooped child listens with head way over on side and ear almost on shoulder, accompanied by a sigh that says, "The whole thing is just too much for me."

5. Natural Child listening often is accompanied by vocalizations such as "Gee," "Um," "Tsk," "Wow" while other person is talking. Head may be cocked with a look of surprise or delight at a new discovery.

Parent listening mimes the manner, opinions, and views of parental figures. Listening in opinionated ways, showing approval and disapproval, is often designed to hook the speaker's NOT OK Child. Even minimal movements and judgmental expressions by listeners may stimulate maximal efforts in the speaker if his Adaptive Child is accessible.

Punishing Parent managers listen with a facial scowl and minimal side-to-side rotation of the head, meaning "I disapprove," "No," and "Don't." They may slump in chair, arms folded across chest, head tilted down, eyes on floor. At this juncture we can expect the speaker's stomach to feel hollow. Repeated rotations of the head show increasing anger, meaning "I wouldn't if I were you," "You can't be serious?" or "You better not." If eyes are narrowed and face flushed, accompanied with clenched rear teeth, an explosion is probably imminent.

The Nurturing Parent listens with his neck arched forward, head tipped down, eyebrows perhaps raised, giving an encouraging and supportive look. Head nodding with a look of guile shows approval of what is being said. Those who spend time in front of groups have observed head-nodding listening which says: "I completely agree with and approve of you." Speaker discomfort with this reaction arises from the suspicion that he is being heard only by the Parent and that there is little contact in the hearer with the subject itself. As with all one-sided relationships, there is little incentive to continue.

The listener has large amounts of social control at his disposal. By powering up his Adult, sitting square in the chair, "listening on the level," and being "straight," he will significantly influence the quality of transactions initiated by the speaker. Not only can he contribute to the stature of the speaker's production, but he can also improve the quality of his own listening perception. Using behavior techniques to expand the use of the Adult contributes to increased rational horsepower of corporate decision-making.

The summary paraphrase is an important communication tool to clarify both speaker's and listener's thinking and to confirm that they are both on the same team. The paraphrase gives the speaker the assurance that the listener is mentally active and the listener the confidence that he is plugged into the right circuits.

By tilting his head and smiling warmly, the listener will bring an angle into his own head and that of the speaker and onlookers as well. The angle or tilt indicates that one ego state in the listener's mind is more heavily weighted than another. If the listener listens from his Punishing Parent, he almost certainly will hook the speaker's NOT OK Child. If the speaker rebels, a fight will ensue and discomfort will be shared around. If the speaker's Complaint Child is hooked, his behavior will suggest that he believes the Punishing Parent, and his speech tones will have an "Indeed, you're absolutely right" quality.

The information-organizing Adult has three functions in listening: (1) He selects from incoming audible material what he deems to be relevant. He compares what's being said with his own opinions, feelings, and knowledge of what is true. He notes which facets may be beneficial to explore more thoroughly later, the general organization and development of the presentation, plus elements of the speaker's behavior that clarify or contradict what he says. (2) He checks what his own ego states have to say about incoming material, plus the relative strength and freedom from contamination of his own Adult. (3) He decides which material to respond to and selects the appropriate behavior. The ability of the listener to successfully perform these functions greatly increases his efficiency in handling daily encounters.

While we commonly suppose that talkers influence listeners, we have already stated that influence also flows in the other direction. There are dynamic ways in which the listener influences the speaker. Managers may not be aware of it, but their listening behavior sways the talker's behavior. Listed below are some common ways that a not-now-talking individual can influence the speaker:

Finger-drumming from either the Rebellious Child or Punishing Parent means "Get to the point."
Shoulder-shrugging means "I don't know and I don't care."
Eye-rolling disdains or discredits speaker.
Cheek-puffing expresses doubt.
Pulling back corners of mouth signifies rejection, disgust, or perhaps "Oh, did I goof!"
Forming hands into a basket, seemingly contemplative, may be prelude to attack.

Head-nodding signifies agreement or disagreement.
Sighs, depending on their length and intensity and whether
they are directed at self or at speaker, have a variety of
meanings. Usually they show tension.
Foot-swishing means "Watch out."
Leg-bouncing means the Rebellious Child has trouble
being compliant and wants to escape.
Expletives or interjections can affect the speaker in different ways. "Tsk, tsk," for example, usually means something is not acceptable.

By becoming more aware of our own and others' listening
behavior, we can importantly improve our ability to communicate with and understand subordinates, colleagues, and
superiors. The application of transactional analysis to listening
states reveals something about speakers' motivations and the
direction in which to work for behavior change in order to
improve an individual's effectiveness. We can learn to control
our listening behavior so that we can influence the speaker in
what we consider to be the most effective way. We can actually
help him communicate better by adopting the following listening behavior.

"Getting level" involves squaring the head and face until a
level-headed posture is achieved. The straightforward attitude
this represents positively affects both listener and speaker. A
level appearance signifies an objective, thoughtful, reasoning
Adult aware of his opinions, feelings, and factual competence.
The on-the-level Adult presents himself directly, without ulterior motives. Such individuals are diligent in approach,
nonopinionated, and compassionate.

Avoiding tilting the head when transacting with another is
part of "getting level." A tilted head shows the presence of a
Parent prejudice or childhood belief to be protected from attack, adhered to, or fought against. Often an angled head together with a mischievous facial expression signals the approval of the "little kid" who is going to disrupt the Adult's
game.

Active listening is a unique skill of the Adult that binds the
sender and receiver in a problem-solving situation. Active listening involves trying to understand what the speaker is feel-

ing or saying. The active listener summarizes what the speaker is saying in his own words and feeds the summary back for the speaker's verification. He reflects back only what he feels the speaker has said—not his own advice, opinions, judgment, analysis, or question. This reduces the possibility of miscommunication. It is part of any helping relationship where the listener accepts responsibility to assist the speaker in the clarification of his own ideas.

Active listening is most appropriate when the speaker's Child tapes are playing. The Child needs to be listened to and affirmed rather than lectured. People free themselves of troublesome feelings, not by avoiding, suppressing, or forgetting them, but by expressing them openly. Because the experience of being heard and understood binds participants, warmth and empathy are part of good listening skills.

"Giving an audible" means being vocally attentive. People prefer vocal stroking to silence. A single vocal stroke is worth six head nods.

"Getting a move on" means increasing the amount of visible movement, including blinking the eyes when listening. Such movement shows the active Adult computing, thinking, and—mainly—responding. On the other hand, if it seems inappropriate to become engaged in a transaction—one that will lead to an argument, for example—simply "lie quiet." Let four to six seconds pass after the speaker has said something to which you do not wish to respond. Complete nonacknowledgment will reduce the likelihood that the speaker will continue in that vein.

In order to listen skillfully, it is necessary for us to make our Adult visible to the speaker. We must learn to listen thoughtfully and objectively. When we take the time and effort to listen skillfully, compassion will be an inherent and obvious part of our transactions.

6

euphoria in decision-making

THERE ARE FEW THINGS more surprising to the student of organizations than the power of a cohesive group to undermine an individual's judgment. Surprise borders on amazement when managers "throw away their brains" and as a group embark on courses of action they would not countenance if they were acting as individuals. Amazement turns to consternation when in the middle of a deteriorating situation, managers appear unable to understand what's happening to them and unwilling to initiate appropriate corrective action.

A New England components manufacturer had long been planning a new corporate headquarters. While only a dozen years old, the firm had cut out a niche in the electronics industry and prospered. From the beginning, it had enjoyed ample space and low rent in a five-story brick structure that had been vacated by a textile manufacturer. As with all older buildings, there was a limit to what remodeling could do. The president and founder of the firm was a strong, forceful man in his mid-fifties who wanted to show his success by erecting an ultramodern edifice. It would, he argued, be attractive to both customers and employees and in the long run pay for itself.

Unfortunately, sales had begun to level off. New competition had entered the field, and there was threat of a competitor's breakthrough with new technology. Costs became an ever-present problem.

Production had introduced some modifications that hadn't worked out well, and certain deliveries had had to be delayed. In one case, loss of a principal customer had upset everyone. In the last year, monthly reports showed operations were marginal, and once or twice the figures on the bottom line appeared in red ink. A miscalculation in labor negotiations had proved more costly than had been anticipated. An 18-month recession had made sales predictions chancy.

Meeting with the executive committee, the president made clear that he understood how the company had misjudged the cost of the new labor contract, miscalculated on the introduction of modifications, and been unable to anticipate the present recession and its effects on customers. "But," he said, "we have faced bigger problems than these. I am confident we can lick this thing. We have talked long enough about the new building. I believe our only course is to move ahead."

One member pulled on his chin, another looked down at the floor doubtfully. It was true their growth at times had seemed miraculous, and they had surprised themselves more than once with what they were able to do. But this was risky business. The committee had a history of friendly relations and going along with the president, who had made them wealthy. When confronted with ideas at variance with his own, the president was known to overlook both idea and person or "to damn him with faint praise." One staff person could be counted on to cheerfully put the best light on things; he generally took the position that if the team worked together and supported the boss in a bold approach, nothing could stop them.

Over the years, the board as a whole enjoyed the perquisites of success and amiable relationships in which differences of opinion were "sanitized." An unspoken agenda forbade members from seriously questioning the positions and actions of another member. Those who disagreed were frowned upon.

When the time came to pass on the new building, it was suggested that if they did not act now, construction costs would only rise again and the moment might be lost. So without serious discussion, the motion passed. Nine months later the company was in receivership and a stockholders' suit was filed against the president. The steel frame ribwork of the new building stands as a monument to another corporate tragedy where managers overtaken by poor process were unable to muster sufficient Adult horsepower to deal with reality.

News media frequently report the consequences of miscalculation—national banks fail, companies enter bankruptcy, the auto market is misjudged, federal agencies license the use of noxious substances, and a country is led into war because politicians misread the intentions and motivations of foreign nationalists—all because of the absence of sound management; all because at critical junctures organizations are underpowered in their Adult.

All such fiascoes are participated in by more or less competent people like ourselves. None of us are immune to the forces that caused others to fail spectacularly. Under what circumstances does group decision-making prove less effective than the decision-making of a competent individual? Some answers can be found by looking closer at group decision-making processes that influence and in some cases control the thinking of individual members.

In any group there are negative processes at work that interfere with mental alertness. Subtle constraints act on members below their level of awareness, preventing them from exercising their critical faculties. Profound NOT OK feelings seem to arise in individuals and to motivate them to become more concerned with retaining the approval of fellow group members than with seeing reality clearly. When under the influence of this concurrence-seeking drive, members evolve hidden agendas to preserve friendly solidarity at the expense of practical and ethical considerations.*

Considering all its aspects, this phenomenon can best be described as group euphoria. It is a shared feeling of invulnerability and righteousness that is groundless, in relation to the situation at hand. When euphoria is present, collective misjudgment can be considered almost a certainty.

In a technological age all save the most Parent managers recognize the peril of one-man decision-making. Research and

---

* There are a number of good sources on decision-making. One which should not be overlooked is Irving L. Janis's *Victims of Groupthink* which inspired many of the ideas in this chapter.

common sense establish the necessity of working collaboratively to reduce the various sources of error that individual
judgment is subject to. A fairly high degree of like-mindedness
on assumptions and values, mutual respect, and skill are pre-
requisites for high-quality decision-making. Group integration
significantly influences productivity. In general, organizational
cohesiveness increases capacity to attract and retain members;
member participation in a group's activity; ability to gain acceptance of group goals as well as of role and task assignments;
member self-esteem, by providing anxiety-reducing security
and stroking; productivity; and comfort level.

However, a too-strong drive for cohesion and concurrence
may cause the quality of group deliberations to deteriorate.
The danger of concurrence-seeking is euphoria in decision-
making. We face a pretzel-shaped question here. How much
we-feeling solidarity is needed to increase the quality of
planning, and how much concurrence-seeking debilitates
rationality? How much Child material is necessary and useful,
and how much contaminates the Adult and separates individuals from reality?

What are the symptoms of group euphoria? How can we
tell when it begins to operate in a group? There are four
telltale signs:

Suppression of personal doubts and illusion of unanimity.
In this process, well documented in social psychology, members suppress unwelcomed points of view by exerting social
pressure on deviating members. First, members increase their
communication with the nonconformist in an attempt to influence him to tone down or revise his dissenting opinion. This
continues only as long as members feel hopeful about changing the nonconformist's mind. If these attempts result in repeated failures, the amount of communication directed toward
the dissenter will decrease markedly. What was at first subtle
disapproval becomes overt, and an exclusion process sets in
that is intended to isolate the nonconformist and restore group
unity. The greater the group cohesion, the stronger the rejection response as members seek to insulate themselves from
disruptive influences.

In a group atmosphere of warm friendliness and convivial-
ity, where members respect each other's opinions and there

are few rewards for critical thinking, some assumptions—of dubious value—may operate:

All members should agree on the questions at hand.
When a group arrives at a unanimous decision, each member feels the group's decision is the only correct one.
Member silence means consent.

Thus critical thinking and reality testing are replaced by the myth of consensual validation. When this happens, group process, often supported by the leader, prevents the surfacing of disagreements and testing of assumptions and data. Areas of convergence are discussed at the expense of areas of divergence which might dirsupt cozy unity. Strokes are exchanged freely, and a general atmosphere of "Nothing can stop us now" arises. When euphoria takes over, each member suppresses his own doubts, frames his questions delicately, and generally exhibits ingratiating behavior.

We assume that most people survive in a stroke-deficient world and that much behavior is powered by NOT OK feelings rooted in earliest infant experiences. Few persons show a strong enough Adult or adequate sense of OK to introduce reality considerations into a group swimming with the euphoric tide. Forthright individuals fall silent when facing peer disapproval for not being sufficiently bold, venturesome, daring. Quickly and powerfully, groups block those who introduce unwanted considerations. Few indeed can withstand the painful NOT OK feelings from group and leader disdain. Still fewer have the motivation to do so when it is so easy to go along with those who demonstrate little concern for reality. There are a thousand rationalizations at hand in the event of failure. Group solidarity tends to increase in direct proportion to external threat.

Ironically, the tendency to suppress individual suspicions and to acquiesce seems to be increased when the group is about to initiate a risky course of action. Presumably when issues are large and consequences grave, the individual's sense of NOT OK is magnified and cohesiveness seems ever more desirable. Because a large number of complex variables may be involved, a relatively unskilled decision-making group underpowered in its Adult may in desperation opt for a less than rational approach. To be underpowered in the Adult means to lack sufficient data, adequate hardware to handle the data, or sufficiently powerful decision-making strategies to compute data at hand.

When matters of great importance are under consideration, a number of forces are at work pressuring for concurrence at the expense of rationality. In the miasma of euphoria, a self-censorship takes place. Individuals minimize their own doubts and suppress counterarguments in order to escape embarrassment. Paradoxically, we find strong forces restraining dissent at the moment that reason is needed most. In an ordinary day, the intelligence of most managers is not tested. Things pretty much run by themselves. The quality of managers' thinking, the content of their minds, and their level of intuition are demonstrated when the pressure is on. Unfortunately, if this is not recognized, increased pressure will be met with increased politics. Instead of improved problem-solving, blaming, games, and maneuvers to escape responsibility are exhibited.

Stereotypical thinking and the dehumanization of opponents. The myth of consensual validation can only be maintained at the expense of ignoring reality. Such oversight is made possible by individuals distorting their view of the situation, opponent, or themselves. The classic way to put distance between ourselves and reality is to create an oversimplified view of the person or situation, a view that is lacking in individual distinguishing marks. This stereotype is repeated without variation. The maintenance of a standardized mental picture shared by all members of a decision-making group is one of the devices of nonreality which encourage euphoria.

Bureaucratic language is a key part of stereotypical thinking. Private, stylized images of reality—often acronyms and shorthand derivatives—when shared around create group fantasy. A military base launches a "Crusade for Peace." New plant construction is heralded as a "New Era for Grand Forks." The annual sales meeting boosts "The Year of the Widgets." Corporate titles are stereotypes. They give us easy "handles" which obviate the need to discover each other as part of the communication process. The president is deemed brighter because of his rank, not because of his tested and proven competence. An assumption such as this on the part of both superiors and subordinates often leads to disaster, because there are no sure correlations between rank and competency at the time of promotions. Too many other variables intervene.

Another tendency that goes hand in hand with stereotyping is that of attributing an impersonal quality to essentially human forces. The process of dehumanization treats human activities as if they were carried out by a force beyond human reason or feeling. If we cross a picket line because we disagree with the union position, we are "scabs" who have been "duped" by the "Communists." Disagreements which might be seen to have a neutral quality have a way of turning into fights.

In a related maneuver, individuals are encouraged to act in behalf of a grand design as though it were not under human control.

For Universal Widget these production schedules must be met.

In the name of all that's holy, we must persevere.

Science demands that we seek facts and leave interpretation to the politicians.

Thus an individual action has its meaning altered by changing the context. What may be morally offensive or ill advised to the individual is legitimated by its relation to a larger organizational reality. Allowing an act to be dominated by its context while denying its human agency and consequences seriously corrodes rationality.

Impersonalizing essentially human forces under the influence of euphoria is one way Parent fantasies corrode the Adult. Another way is to devalue the opponent or victim prior to or as a consequence of action against him. Devaluation of the "victim" almost always accompanies destructive behavior against him: "He's just stupid and got what he deserved." In some cases the devaluation may be concerted and systematic.

We have all known individuals, groups, and even divisions that seem unable to please management by anything they do. All efforts are viewed as inadequate and all corrections as ineffectual. This is a situation which all managers recognize, many fear, and with which few are able to cope. An individual's NOT

OK feelings being what they are, he too often accepts such derogations by the rest of the group members. The here-and-now manager spots those leftover Parent generalizations which do not represent reality, and does not let them stand unchallenged. By demythologizing stereotypes, we strengthen the individual and collective Adults of the organization.

Having acted against the victim, managers often find it necessary to view him as a substandard performer, whose punishment was inevitable, given his deficiencies of character, reason, or whatever. Such managers cannot feel good when behaving this way. A behaviorally trained manager will recognize that the game "Gotcha" arises out of bad feelings and devaluation of the opponent. Bad feelings come first, then aggressive behavior, then rationalization of the behavior. A behaviorally trained manager "owns" his own behavior. He doesn't claim that others cause or are responsible for his behavior. If he derogates others, he's the one doing it. He doesn't argue that the victim caused him to act in this way. Distinguishing behavior that arises out of internal needs from that which is responsive to external reality makes dehumanization of opponents impossible.

Uncritical belief in group's inherent morality, with efforts to rationalize deviant data. When euphoria interferes with individual mental alertness, a group may exhibit a high degree of self-satisfaction and a shared sense of moral rightness about their decisions. This is exhibited in a disinclination to raise ethical issues. An individual can make himself unwelcome by calling into question the assumed high-mindedness and morality of an action under consideration. Lack of clarity on ethical issues is a major contributor to organizational dysfunction, as Lockheed has painfully been made aware. Morally weak positions are rationally unsupportable. Practical people are going to have to undertake the hard work of clarifying their moral positions if they are to prove adequate to contemporary challenges.

A process of natural selection works to create a moral homogeneity among management groups. Over the years those who are too "different" are factored out by the promotion process and individuals arrive at positions of responsibility who share the same values and beliefs. The likelihood of someone raising questions about these values and beliefs is minimal. Furthermore, managers even when not influenced by euphoria are likely to firmly resist challenges to their assumptions about themselves and their organizations. Most resistant are the justifications for the behavior that brought them to their present prominence. Parent leaders are often coercive, and their weapons for putting down challenges have been honed to lethal effectiveness. To the unwary, assertiveness passes as knowledge.

Embarrassment seems to be the most upsetting emotion individuals face and fear. It is the motive power for avoidance behavior. Going against the social grain is too painful for most individuals. The more important the relationship, the greater the fear and the less likelihood of raising difficult issues. Being discredited hooks the whole load of childhood NOT OK and powers the drive for concurrence and compliance. This ability of the Adaptive Child to dismantle both sound Parent morality and Adult reality is a source of consternation for all planners.

When Child feelings contaminate the Adult, it functions at reduced capacity and exhibits two dysfunctions, denial and distortion. Denial is the refusal to accept or acknowledge the reality or validity of a phenomenon even when its truth has been demonstrated. Distortion is the altering or changing that falsifies essentially true facts or ideas. By selecting and believing only facts and ideas in accord with the group position, the participant encourages euphoria. He also escapes the hard work of getting into the here-and-now of problem-solving.

Rationalization is the finding of reasons for doing and believing what we want to do and believe anyhow. It's a technique that allows us to find reasons to justify our behavior and encourage its continuance. Making emotional preferences appear to be rational conclusions is a form of self-deceit and fantasy useful in maintaining a friendly group climate.

One of the most disquieting effects of an out-of-control Child ego state is its ability to impair the Parent. Great business fiascoes that become great legal struggles occur when reason and morality are abandoned. Some of the saddest episodes in business history occur as a consequence of managers' abandoning both legal and ethical considerations. When justice and reason catch up with them, invariably the retort is:

"I was only following orders and doing what everyone else did."

The most clear and present danger to executive groups is not an individual's selfish impulses but his drive for concurrence. This is what is involved in Eric Hoffer's concept of the "true believer." An individual who trades his moral and rational identity for integration into corporate security vitiates his potential for excellence.

Illusion of invulnerability. As mentioned above, groups often take riskier actions than individuals. People operating out of the Child ego state stimulate each other, and there is a general rising emotional effect. This may be manifested in extreme group optimism and a sense of unlimited future. As emotion takes over, there is a tendency to leave reality behind, and an illusion of invulnerability is shared around. Once euphoria takes hold, it captivates all. Adults present are reluctant to undertake the unpleasant task of critically assessing the limits of group power. Often limits are discovered only after groups get in over their financial heads.

Along with the feeling of invulnerability may appear boundless admiration for the leader. His ideas are heard with special clarity and deemed to be inordinately trenchant. It is easy to focus the shared sense of rightness and well-being on a supposed charisma of the leader. Since childhood, parent figures have been seen as benign and the source of wisdom and protection. The Child in us anticipates resolution of problems through the intervention of a charismatic leader. Hero worship is a common strategy whereby we associate ourselves with the good qualities, real or assumed, in others. We identify with our heroes. It's so much easier than mobilizing our Adult and taking what responsibility we can for the problem.

Irving L. Janis, in his study of four federal decision-making fiascoes (*Victims of Groupthink*), points out that in groups where the drive for concurrence is powerful someone will appoint himself "mindguard." The mindguard arrogates to himself the role of protecting the group and its leaders from inimical information that would call into question tacit assumptions about the group's effectiveness and morality. Whereas a bodyguard protects against physical assaults, the mindguard seeks to keep adverse information from the group that would shatter their complacency and invite a painful or disturbing reevaluation of policies.

When an action has begun, or a course been undertaken, that is not promising, the group may protect the leader and themselves from the unwelcome news by sounding the note: "There is no turning back, the decision has been made. Now everyone's task is to support the leader." Loyalty to the leader is placed above problem-solving as members seek to protect him from the unhappy truth. Once the plan is launched, there may be a dulling of sensitivity to reality. This in the long run does the greatest disservice to the leader. As the situation deteriorates, all participants find it harder to ask the reality questions.

Situational and spatial factors, such as those suggesting status and power, may contribute to isolation from reality. When surroundings suggest power and affluence, unwary individuals may internalize external attributes and allow themselves to enjoy a low sense of vulnerability to the consequences of their actions and proceed on a course more hazardous than is warranted. Fantasy feeds euphoria. Such fantasizing is one more testimony to the power of the NOT OK feelings with which we seek to cope. Since fantasy opportunities are limited, they are well-nigh irresistible. Reality has a way of putting things straight. Aware of the seductiveness of power, the thoughtful manager works skillfully to reduce euphoria and return deliberations to reality-based considerations. In this, the manager's task is not easy.

How do these four symptoms or causes—in fact, they are both—of social conformity function? What is operating when we-feeling is running high and members exhibit more concern for mutual support than for problem-solving of reality questions? Behind the pressure for concurrence are attempts to avoid NOT OK feelings and possible loss of self-esteem resulting from alienation of the group. We assume that most people struggle against negative feelings originally caused by the radical dependency of infancy and more or less unfriendly rearing practices. These feelings, operating below conscious awareness, are the motive force for most non–reality-based behavior. Fight or flight is the characteristic response to internal NOT OK feelings and it takes place apart from reality issues that the group faces.

The "I'M NOT OK" half of our life position is based on the immediate evidence of experienced bad feelings. The "YOU'RE OK" half derives from the good things we experienced from our parents. This felt-decision that good things come from others is the reason acceptance by OK others becomes the central support of our own sense of self-worth. When the group has senior rank, membership has special allure. All the fantasies of special honors accruing to senior membership pursued for years cannot easily be risked, even for reality. Managers with the greatest affiliative needs may ascend by fraternal, rather than competency, considerations. Facing the harsher reality of senior management problems, they may find themselves underpowered in their Adult and controlled by their concurrence needs.

We all know of cases where the needs of the organization, the demands of reality, and the imperatives of morality were unwittingly sacrificed to the gratification needs of senior management. Unable to face the hard work of firing up the Adult, researching and defining problems, lining up alternatives and weighing probabilities, individuals opt for cozy amiability and an "Oh, what the hell" attitude. The Child becomes reckless and joins with his peers to overextend the organization's capabilities and embark on risky courses. Euphoria replaces problem-solving and everyone has fun.

When we watch a euphoric group acting on its omnipotent fantasies, it becomes clear that their behavior originates more in unresolved issues in each member's past and less in response to challenges from the environment. In fantasy the euphoric group, now regressed to rebellious children, respond to threats with an obscene finger gesture.

It is important to know how to prevent euphoria—and thus prevent costly miscalculations and folly in decision-making—while utilizing the benefits of group solidarity, because today more decisions of consequence are made within the group context than in any other setting. The practical issue is how resources in the team can be utilized to ensure the best decisions the team is capable of making.

Managers, by and large, are in the dark about how to effectively use the groups they are dependent upon. They proceed on the basis of intuition, custom, and bias, rather than on systematic principles of group life. Lack of full awareness of group dynamics, coupled with an unsystematic approach to their use, and the absence of positive experience contribute to the uneasy feelings of many managers as they entrust their decision dilemmas to teams. The cynicism of these managers is expressed in such remarks as "A camel is a horse created by a committee" and "If you want a job done, do it yourself. If you don't want it done give it to a committee."

One of the earliest and most consistent research findings is the effect of statistical contributions to team decisions. The research of Jay Hall at the University of Texas was presented in the summer of 1968 at the NTL program for specialists in organizational development at Bethel, Me. The NASA game has proved to be the classic simulation involving the use of consensus. The assumption of the familiar axiom "Two heads are better than one" reflects a common-sense notion that group decision-making ensures a more adequate decision than if an individual struggles to a decision alone. It works, apparently because of the cancellation of individual errors of reason, judgment, or passion. Extreme judgments tend to cancel out one another so that neither excessively bad nor extremely good judgments are reflected in the final decision.

Hall's research indicates that the numerical average of individual decisions, when decision tasks are quantifiable, is superior to more than one-half of the individual decisions contained in that average. This finding reveals something about the accuracy of individual judgments. The normal bell curve distribution that suggests 50 percent would be better and 50 percent worse than the average scores does not hold. The finding that the average decision is superior to more than one-half of the individual scores tells us that the majority of individuals fall toward the inaccuracy end of a display of individual decisions. Decisions produced by groups that interact in reaching a decision, as opposed to the noninteraction of statistical averaging techniques, are superior to both the majority of individual decisions contributing to the average and the statistical averaging of individual decisions.

Further, there is much data indicating that the kind of transactions a group employs exerts significant influence on the quality of the final decision. Therefore, managers who understand the consequences of Parent, Adult, and Child transactions are equipped to improve the quality of the group process and the final decision.

Each of the following decision-making techniques has a different cause-and-effect relationship to group performance.

◻ *Minority control technique.* Decisions are made by individuals and/or a minority faction of the group.

◻ *Majority vote technique.* Decisions are based on the support of a majority of group members.

◻ *Consensus.* Decisions are based on the equal support and agreement of the total membership.

Compared with the other techniques, decisions based on minority control are the least adequate, particularly today, when problems are complex and change is rapid. When the number of persons contributing to a decision is decreased, the final decision depends more on individual member competency than on interaction effects. Managers are increasingly unwilling to depend on "hot shots." In addition to reduced quality of decision products, there are losses in energy and in positive effects on motivation. The majority of individual judgments, it will be remembered, are less accurate than the decisions of the "average individual." Thus chance factors work against the effectiveness of this technique.

The majority vote technique is superior to minority control because it benefits from both statistical effects and interaction contributions. Since at least a medium amount of interaction involving a majority, if not all, of group members is necessary to achieve majority agreement, a variety of positive effects accruing from interaction may be reflected in the final group decision. The disadvantage is that a portion of the benefits inherent in well-executed interaction may be missing. For instance, if the out-voted minority are unable to influence the final decision, all interaction effects are not brought to the service of the decision.

Consensus is a decision-making strategy wherein all group members share equally in and are responsible for the final decision. No decision becomes final which does not get the approval of every group member. However, personal approval of a decision need not be total and complete; a member can give his consent to a decision that he feels is the best one possible under the circumstances, while remaining doubtful of its adequacy. For an inexperienced group, consensus may be impossible to obtain. It requires that members have a fairly sophisticated understanding of ego states, transactional and game dynamics, and the distribution and use of power in organizations. Experience indicates that consensus results in decisions of superior quality along any measurable dimension.

Paradoxically, consensus is the least-used form of decision-making. The more mechanical techniques of minority control and majority vote are most favored. These are used in order to avoid conflict which results from differences of opinion. In instances where fairly dramatic power differences exist among members, minority control may be employed to short-circuit conflict, overcome group inertia, and save time. In such a case the cost/benefit ratio must indicate whether organizational change in the direction of openness and consensus is warranted. Whether the aim is to reduce euphoria or other interaction deficiencies in decision-making, the strategy is the same: raise the skill level of managers at each level of responsibility. A deliberate program designed to improve organizational effectiveness would include the following:

Behavior training. Behavior training sharpens an individual's participation capabilities. The goal is to enable each manager to put his Adult in charge of his behavior. When he can do that, he makes the greatest contributions to the organization. Such training takes time, consistent top-management support, and extensive follow-up. The goals of such a program are:

Unhooking from the NOT OK past.
Liberation of rationality.
Increased interpersonal skill.
Improved stroking and sense of OK.
Clearer problem analysis through strengthened Adult ego
   state.
Reduction of miscommunication and dissonance.
Greater self-management.
Cessation of game playing.

Process management. Process management strategies assign responsibility to all members of an organization to be aware not simply of problem content but of the resolution process as well. The key assumption here is that if people don't grow, organizations can't grow. The two types of growth are interdependent. The strategy is to change not people, but the organization's reward system so that it reinforces productive, and not counterproductive, behavior. The technique usually identified with this is team building, the goals of which are (1) to create an open climate throughout the organization; (2) to supplement the authority of role and status with that of competence; (3) to maximize collaboration and reduce destructive fight and game playing; (4) to push decision-making downward in the organization; (5) to create ownership of organizational objectives throughout the company; (6) to develop a reward system that supports the growth both of people and the organization; and (7) to build and maintain trust.

Improved decision-making skills. The increasing complexity of problems means an increasing number of variables have to be considered in decision-making. Indeed, some problems can only be approached through the use of electronic data processing machines. There are times when managers have the facts before them and they have to estimate probabilities about the future and choose one course over another. In recent years a great deal of work has been done in the field of planning and decision-making practices. Here is a list of good decision-making practices:

Develop as complete a list of alternatives as possible.

Establish mid-course evaluation points.

Develop contingency plans that become operative when unforeseen events intervene.

Explore thoroughly alternatives for drawbacks and risks both obvious and not obvious.

Use outside experts whenever possible for new insight and data.

Manage decision-making process in such a way as to avoid pitfalls of euphoria, overcontrol, and so on.

Use alternative strategies such as subgroups, parallel track teams, and "exception" sessions.

The more rigorous the process, the greater the likelihood of an adequate decision.

Value clarification. Values are functional. Most organizations would benefit from undertaking the hard work of describing and defining their purpose and goals and implementing their values. Many managers do not have a clear idea of these organizational aspects, and often there is dissonance between belief and practice.

I see evidence that firms which are most explicit about democratic values are proving themselves best able to deal with change. Any effort a company makes toward this end in nonturbulent times will stand it in good stead during crisis. In the technological age, rationalism will be tempered by the spirit and philosophy of humanism and the subtler dynamics of the human spirit.

7

life positions
and management style

WHEN MANAGERS first encounter life positions, they have an "aha" experience. The light goes on. Things they hadn't understood before now make sense. Life position is best identified by an individual's objective observation of his own behavior and the outcomes of his transactions. A reaction of surprise is not uncommon when the individual undertakes this dispassionate assessment in his Adult.

For most, one life position, I'M NOT OK—YOU'RE OK, will be dominant day in and day out. Certain situations may occasionally revive an individual's latent secondary position and infrequently a single person may experience all four positions within a given time frame.

A life position is an individual's basic attitude toward life and other people. It was assumed in his earliest years (as discussed in Chapter 1). Whether he realized it or not, this life decision became the basis of his attitude toward his co-workers and transactions with them. The material upon which this fundamental decision was made was often confused and disorganized, arising from all three ego states, but particularly from the Parent and the Child.

This is where the negative ideas about the self originate, those bad feelings that we carry through life that make life "heavy" and create feelings of "depression." It is this pressure which bends our minds in certain ways. It keeps us walking well-worn tracks, unwilling to take on the added "heat" of risks, new adventure, and self-examination. Bad feelings about others can be modified by positive experiences with OK people. It is more difficult to modify bad feelings about the self, because all transactions are selectively viewed to support the original NOT OK decision. People seem to be able to believe anything they desire.

The major source of trouble comes from the parents' Parent ego states. Their rationalizations are many and seemingly perfect: "You can't start too soon to teach infants the difference between right and wrong." "The pain of discipline now will bring the pleasure of competence later." The Parent always makes sense to himself in terms of his own life position. Therefore, he feels justified in laying his views on those in his control. And no one is more in his control than his own children.

From the young child's point of view, parents are the one and only source of life and its good experiences. Parents don't have to insist to be believed by the child. A parent's insistence only reinforces the positions, and of course there is the implicit threat of rejection or punishment if the child rebels. The child gets the idea, on the unconscious level, that something enormous would be wrong if he did not adopt the parent's position with regard to, well, all the important things of life. Because they internalize parent material, children behave like their parents, often seek marriage partners reminiscent of the parents, and often maintain the same social and political outlook.

When external events do not correspond with the child's set, he doesn't conclude that something new and fresh is approaching. He concludes that something is wrong. In effect, the child holds a position, and anything different is wrong. The child, and later the grown-up, is predisposed to keep things the same: "My position right or wrong, because it's my position." The inability to hold their life position up to the evidence of objective reality is the source of dysfunction in Parent-dominant managers. In the most literal sense, they seldom get to the problem. They have all their answers before the problem is defined.

This is where the great word "permission" comes in. The

YOU'RE OK WITH ME

Problem-solving manager	Friendly Persuasive manager
High-pressure manager	Unconscious manager

I'M OK
WITH ME

I'M NOT OK
WITH ME

YOU'RE NOT OK WITH ME

Figure 8. Management styles model.

individual can give himself permission to think and behave in ways he hasn't been open to before. He can tentatively approach a new idea even though it doesn't seem to fit his own views. He can try it on for size. If it doesn't work, he can discard it. If it makes some sense and opens up other new insights, he can tentatively take the next step. By identifying and understanding his life position, a manager gains mastery over his life goals and behavior.

By giving himself permission to live a little, he may start seeing things as they are for the first time. He may for the first time explore those ideas, directions, attitudes, and behaviors that express his uniqueness. He can stop living life as others saw it and thought he should see it and begin to discover what it can be for himself. His thinking doesn't have to be second-hand. It can be authentically his.

At the conclusion of an encounter, no matter how many transactions have taken place, the outcome can be categorized in one of four different ways. The diagram in Figure 8 is based on the four life positions.* In the cells of the diagram,

---

* The management styles model and descriptions are based on the unpublished ideas of my good friend and mentor Ted Jackson, Ph.D., of Scarsdale, New York.

types of managers are identified, based on how they feel about themselves and how they feel about others.

The High-Pressure Manager

Operating out of the I'M OK—YOU'RE NOT OK life position, this individual attempts to support himself by diminishing others. He exhibits controlling behavior. His actions say, "I don't care about you."

> *Boss:* Well, that's the story for next year. We're going to have to stretch to make it. I'm confident I can count on you to make a maximum effort. If you have any problems, buck them up through channels. I look forward to hearing about your good work. Any questions?
>
> *Salespeople:* Good show, boss.

I'M OK—YOU'RE NOT OK is the life position of the distrustful individual.* He keeps distance between himself and others. It usually results because the individual was brutalized by adults when he was small and helpless. When his parents approached him, he suffered pain. When he was left to himself to "lick his wounds," he gave himself strokes and felt better. The ordinary course of things is reversed here. When the parents approach, the child experiences discomfort, and when they leave, things get better for him. So he concludes, I'M OK—YOU'RE NOT OK. This is the survivor, who has learned how to be tough. He received his training from his parents. He spends his energy avoiding or getting rid of other people.

For this child there are no OK people. But having made that decision, he suffers from stroke deprivation. Because he is highly defended, he is unable to receive the support and caring which might relieve this self-defeating position. His Adult is underpowered and unable to objectify the situation to discover his own complicity in it. Only when he comes to understand the source and consequences of his life position will he

---

* Chapter 3 of *I'm OK—You're OK* has an excellent discussion of life positions to which my debt is obvious.

be able to seek those strokes which could create a life of new possibilities for him.

The high-pressure manager (Figure 9) comes off the wrong end of his feelings. His distancing behavior has just the opposite consequence of what he needs. Basically unfriendly, his domineering and manipulative behavior maintains his original life position. This is the way in which a life position is determinative. The individual makes everything fit his original decision about life and others. He uses rituals, games, and withdrawal to sterilize his transactions with others. He manipulates from the top-dog position. His games are likely to include "Gotcha," "Let's You and Him Fight," "Why Don't You . . . Yes, But," "Blemish," and "Uproar." He does not seek technical knowledge because he doesn't feel he needs it. Control, not insight, is his concern. Surviving, not problem-solving, is his goal.

Because this individual is basically unfriendly, his co-workers would just as soon avoid contact with him. He is the

---

Basic behavior
Forceful one-way communication, pressure, smoothness, games, and gimmicks.

People involved
Other managers and subordinates serve as objects.

Technical knowledge required
Little needed; exaggerates, is evasive in answering questions; bluffs, misleads.

Attitude of manager
Basically unfriendly, domineering, and exploiting.

Attitude of co-workers
Evasive, unfriendly, minimizes contact.

Resultant development in manager
Increased alienation; becomes an isolate.

Figure 9. The high-pressure manager.

subject of much gossip. He becomes increasingly isolated from both co-workers and organizational problems. As this happens, there may be further behavior deterioration.

In his relations with others the I'M OK—YOU'RE NOT OK individual proceeds on the assumption that agreement is impossible and conflict inevitable. The argument runs like this: Since there are no OK people, I can't trust anyone to do any more than vigorously promote his own self-interest. I can't expect others to value my concerns. I can't expect others to work collaboratively, except temporarily when it suits their best interest and until they can again assert their dominance. In a world of limited possibilities, I shouldn't be surprised if others make gains at my expense. That's part of the game. I can't expect others to live ethically, or to believe in the objective reality of reason.

With these assumptions, conflict is inevitable. Experience has taught this man that attack is the best defense. Always keep them off balance. Such a manager assembles a retinue of "straw" men and women to do his bidding. When he calls them "Yes men" he identifies the plastic nature of their strokes. He arranged it that way, as he had to arrange for his own stroking as an infant. Yet the more obsequious his functionaries are, the more he will despise them, which may eventually lead to their replacement.

The creation of artificial feelings of friendship, anger, caring, or whatever is called by Berne a racket. Rackets are ways of making things come out as they always have in the past. Sometime in early childhood the individual selects, from all the feelings he has experienced, the one which works best for him. Although he considers the feeling natural, in fact it is artificial. Like a manipulative role, a racket is a manipulative feeling manufactured for the benefits that can be obtained. It is a creation of the self-indulgent Child and not an authentic response to objective reality. It may be the payoff of a game, or the individual can create the unauthentic feeling by himself. One who indulges in synthetic feelings of hurt, anger, fear, or guilt for their manipulative value is called a racketeer. If an individual feels guilty about some behavior and does not stop it, that's a racket. If the behavior were an authentic and spontaneous response to real life, the individual would be in his Natural Child.

Racket feelings mask and substitute for the more basic NOT OK feelings. Only the pseudo-feeling is permitted and acknowledged. Rackets are not always easy to identify. One can suspect a racket when there is insufficient cause for the display of anger. When irritation breaks through a facade of composure, one may suspect that the friendliness was manufactured. Excessive friendliness without sufficient reason may cause one to wonder whether the feeling is real or manufactured. In order to find out, it is necessary to look back to the individual's earliest years. If his parents insisted on respect and "honor" even when abusing the child, in later life he may be confused as to whether he feels angry or caring toward his parents. He may have manufactured the necessary respectful attitude. His racket feeling of being respectful may make it difficult for him to express real caring.

Some managers cope with feelings of fear, or even of caring, by displaying anger. Anger for them is permissible and fear is not, so they substitute one for the other. Of course, they may truly get angry if others aggress back. The racket nature of anger can be seen when the individual fuels the fires of resentment long after the occasion which produced it is over. Subordinates minimize contact and take cover when the boss is manufacturing his familiar mood. Because of their ability to exploit others, high-pressure managers may consider themselves effective at their jobs. It is difficult not to get manipulated into their rackets and games; it takes a sound, fully conscious Adult.

In group transactions, the high-pressure manager tends to play win-lose games (Figure 10). For him things have a way of degenerating into fight. Issues tend to flatten out and lose their complexity. Individuals tend to lose their identity and become blurred into "them and us." When this happens, lines tend to harden and the chances for intelligent problem resolution fade. The only hope then is for a third-party resolution. A judge or arbitrator settles the dispute, using one of a variety of compromise formulas. Since this is a painful and frustrating pro-

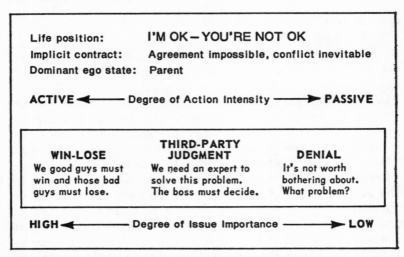

Life position:	**I'M OK – YOU'RE NOT OK**
Implicit contract:	Agreement impossible, conflict inevitable
Dominant ego state:	Parent

ACTIVE ◄────── Degree of Action Intensity ──────► **PASSIVE**

| **WIN-LOSE** | **THIRD-PARTY JUDGMENT** | **DENIAL** |
| We good guys must win and those bad guys must lose. | We need an expert to solve this problem. The boss must decide. | It's not worth bothering about. What problem? |

HIGH ◄────── Degree of Issue Importance ──────► **LOW**

Figure 10. The high-pressure manager: basic assumptions in handling interpersonal and group transactions.

cess, it becomes necessary, whenever possible, to ignore problems, hoping they may resolve themselves.

The Friendly-Persuasive Manager

Operating out of the I'M NOT OK—YOU'RE OK life position, this individual copes by being friendly and avoiding trouble.

> *Worker:* Good to see you. Hey, I wonder if you can give me some help on the Larder contract. I like your ideas.
>
> *Co-worker:* You know more about that than I do. You know you can count on me to do anything I can to help you. But I'm really not up on those technical matters. I wonder if Sam wouldn't be more help to you?

That sparring could go on for some time before they got to the worker's question. In this transaction, the co-worker is trying to get rid of the worker while at the same time keeping up appearances of affability. It's too much trouble to get into the subject, and the co-worker has a NOT OK position to maintain.

Basic behavior
Cultivates friendships, is entertaining, good listener, and joiner.

People involved
Everyone required to get job done.

Technical knowledge required
Used selectively as a tool to impress others.

Attitude of manager
Affable, personally engaging, compliant; stresses loyalty, "win him over."

Attitude of co-workers
Friendly but wary; "Hold him off."

Resultant development in manager
Increased skill in dealing with people.

Figure 11. The friendly-persuasive manager.

Most people decide as small children, before their Adult has had an opportunity to develop, that I'M NOT OK—YOU'RE OK is the only life position that makes sense. NOT OK was the adaptation to the accumulated negative and often chaotic experience of the helpless infant. The size and unavailability of the parent contributed to this. It is a felt rather than a thought decision. It is deterministic. It can be changed but not before it is understood.

One way individuals cope with this is by achieving the strokes that come from affability and achievement. Friendly-persuasive managers (Figure 11) value the skills of friendliness and of being a good listener and team player. They cultivate and value friendships and associations which help them get ahead. Technical knowledge is used selectively as a tool to impress and influence others. Stressing loyalty and being a good fellow, they are pleasant companions who tend to avoid tough problems or to discuss them in a jocose manner. Their hyperfriendliness may cause co-workers to be cautious and to wait to see what happens when push comes to shove. Often their backup behavior is Punishing Parent. Game playing is a prominent part of those functioning out of their NOT OK Child. "Harried," "Wooden Leg," "Gee You're Wonderful," and "Ain't It Awful" are their typical games.

When transacting with others, the friendly-persuasive manager assumes that complete agreement probably is not possible, but that if everyone acts civilly, things can go forward with as little friction as possible (Figure 12). He does not expect agreement because he does not appreciate or know how to utilize the power of reason. Having closed that door, his next best option is to make things as comfortable as possible for himself and others.

Managers in this NOT OK life position can cope in an alternate way. Because they feel low, powerless, and depressed, they may spend energy in avoiding themselves, others, and the daily business of taking charge of their life. Being with OK people may be painful. In group transactions, if at all possible, this manager will seek to avoid the problem. In some cases he may express provocative behavior, so that others turn on him. One consequence of rebellious behavior is that the group will eventually attempt to isolate him. This negative consequence is not unsought since it maintains the original life position.

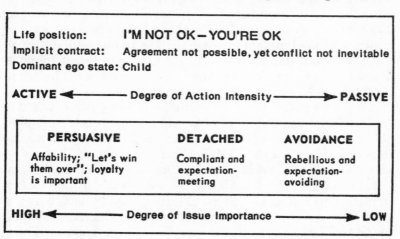

Figure 12. The friendly-persuasive manager: basic assumptions in handling interpersonal and group transactions.

More often this NOT OK manager will maintain his affable and compliant demeanor while attempting to remain detached from the action. If action becomes intense and the issues important, he will bring his social and integrating skills to bear. His strategy is "Let's win them over." He seeks to maintain an attitude of loyalty to friends and the organization. His coping strategy is: If people, particularly important people, like me, I must be OK.

Such gains are short-lived, however. They do not produce either happiness or a sense of lasting worth because they deal with the symptom only, not the basic life position. First the NOT OK life position must be uncovered and discarded and the OK position put in its place, and then authentic feelings can replace rackets and games. And, next, the individual can liberate bound energy—which had been spent on maintaining the NOT OK past—for use by his Adult for problem-solving present matters.

The Unconscious Manager

The individual who operates out of the I'M NOT OK— YOU'RE NOT OK life position is not often seen in business organizations. He will have selected himself out. He does not have sufficient Adult appropriable to function in social situations. Almost all people have genius potential, but as with a calculator, nothing happens until you turn it on. If stroking disappears altogether after the infant learns to walk, because his "babying" days are over; if mother is cold; if punishments are harsh and frequent—somewhere in the third year the child will conclude I'M NOT OK—YOU'RE NOT OK. This life position is characterized by despair. The individual simply gives up seeking strokes. Totally unconscious, he simply exists. The position is hard to relieve because all experience is selectively interpreted to support it.

The unconscious manager operates on the assumption that agreement is not possible and that conflict is inevitable (Figure 13). Consequently he gets nowhere with life and other people. Because his Adult is excluded, he gives up seeking strokes. Then the streams of his emotional life dry up, leaving a desert of futility. This causes further behavioral regression. It is not

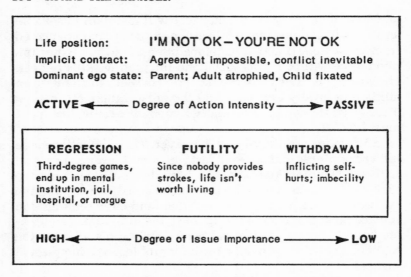

Figure 13. The unconscious manager: basic assumptions in handling interpersonal and group transactions.

unlikely for such an unfortunate individual to end up in jail, a hospital, or the morgue.

The Problem-Solving Manager

Operating out of the I'M OK—YOU'RE OK position, this manager achieves real success in his work. He is able to get on with the business of life. Freed from his own NOT OK feelings, he is able to find, and build on, the OK in others. Because his intelligence is operating to understand the source of the original NOT OK, he decides to test the I'M OK—YOU'RE OK hypothesis.

There is a qualitative difference between the first three positions and the fourth one. The first three are unconscious feeling adaptations made early in life. The fourth, OK, position is based on thought. It is not limited by the individual's personal experience. It is the only rational and productive position that functions in the here-and-now. Much empirical testing will be necessary before an individual can fully accept this reality. The NOT OK recording continues to play, causing the old distress to recur. However, the Adult, now able to distinguish feeling from reason and from opinions, can unhook without being trapped in the continuing circle of self-defeating behavior.

People free themselves to live their own lives when they understand the predicament of the first three positions and how current behavior can perpetuate it. Instead of being controlled by the rigidities of the Parent or the negative feelings derived from early childhood, the individual puts his intelligence in control of his behavior and can function, fully conscious, in the here-and-now. With the Adult as executive of the personality, he begins to put new and successful material into his core storage, which to some degree replaces the troublesome material of childhood.

The basic behavior of the problem-solving manager is being open to share all relevant information about the problem (Figure 14). This includes not only his own opinions, feelings,

Basic behavior
Cooperative problem-solving, openly sharing all relevant information.

People involved
Everyone needed to solve problems using values, feelings, and intelligence.

Technical knowledge required
Used as needed to best solve problems.

Attitude of manager
Reality-grounded, authentically friendly, and fact-minded.

Attitude of co-workers
Welcome him as real source of help.

Resultant development in manager
Committed to his own growth; increased interpersonal and problem-solving skills plus mental flexibility, growing self-acceptance.

Figure 14. The problem-solving manager.

intuitions, and reason, but also his insights into the processes and dynamics of his own organization. He determinedly avoids the duplicity of secrecy, manipulative roles, rackets, and games and attempts to transact with individuals in real time. He is free to take the risks and enjoy the benefits of authentic encounter. He is committed to strengthening the human resource of his organization and to getting out of others' way so they can get to the problems.

He employs technical knowledge to solve problems, wary of its claims to be a panacea. He is reality-grounded, authentically friendly, and fact-minded. He practices the mental skill of ferreting out the small amount of wheat from the chaff of most communications. He holds on to what he knows until better evidence is produced. Because he is thoughtful and reflective, he can be counted on to separate the material and immaterial.

Co-workers welcome this person's help on any problem. He can be counted on to support them personally and at the same time to engage the issue critically. He can be counted on to do his homework on a problem and to not talk off the top of his head. This manager is committed to being fully conscious. His own growth is a personal ideal. He is wary of his own prejudices and understands how his NOT OK feelings can block his intelligence. He finds that he is increasingly comfortable within himself. The problem-solving manager is:

□ Committed to his own growth and aware of his expanding consciousness
□ Skillful at problem-solving techniques, including EDP and mathematical software
□ Successful at giving help to others that promotes their growth
□ Open to sharing information about himself and about the problem
□ Comfortable in groups, where he is able to reflect on and experiment with ideas; and deal with concepts analytically, associatively, and constructively
□ Determined to end the duplicity of rackets, games, and manipulative roles in his organization

The problem-solving manager increases the rational horse-power of decision-making in his organization (Figure 15). The I'M OK—YOU'RE OK position opens up new possibilities that are denied those laboring under NOT OK feelings. When working on a problem, his implicit contract with co-workers is that agreement is possible although there will be disagreements on the way. He works for consensus, and while he doesn't always achieve it, he seldom experiences team members who aren't 100 percent behind the effort. He doesn't allow issues to fester below the surface; he unearths and deals with them openly.

Things run smoothly in this manager's organization. There are no unwelcome surprises. In issues of middle-level intensity, he can be counted on to bargain toward a resolution and to never over- or undersolve a problem. When problems are compelling and the pressure intense, he goes for the facts, scrutinizing data, searching for alternatives, weighing probabilities, and using all resources available to arrive at a decision. It is just for this kind of work that years were invested in building a sound organization—for authentic people.

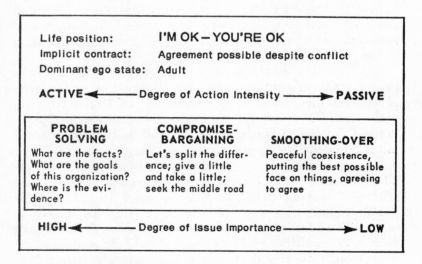

Figure 15. The problem-solving manager: basic assumptions in handling interpersonal and group transactions.

script behavior
and equal opportunity
for women

IT IS WITH A SENSE OF RELIEF that a manager concerned about the consequences of the unequal treatment of women and minorities welcomes the arrival of governmental intervention in the problem.

By executive order and statute the government has acted to prohibit management practices that discriminate on the basis of race, religion, color, sex, or national origin. Under Title VII of the Civil Rights Act of 1964, the Equal Employment Opportunity Commission was established, and in 1972 it received full legal powers to investigate and seek legal redress in those cases where companies were not able to prove effective compliance with the purpose and intent of the code. Already some relatively dramatic events have taken place. In 1973 a major public utility was assessed $30 million in back pay to minorities and women, and another $45 million the following year. A major airline was assessed $24 million for flight attendants who, it was proven, had been systematically barred from promotion.

This is an area of considerable sensitivity for the average company and its managers. There seems to be almost a revolution taking place in relationships between sexes. Understanding script behavior, where it comes from, and its consequences may give us some insights into sexism. At the same time it will prepare us to better meet the challenges presented by the struggle for equality.

It can be noticed that people seem to do the same thing over and over as if controlled by a computer in their heads, and that they will continue to act this way no matter how disastrous the results. They seem unable to understand or respond to the fresh opportunities each day presents. They are, in fact, rigid and compulsive—just the opposite of authentic and autonomous. Almost all human activity is preprogrammed by unconscious decisions made in early childhood. It is as if we participated in writing a script when we were children that we would follow the rest of our lives. When this happens life becomes a melodrama where authenticity, awareness, and intimacy are impossible.

The term "script" is apt because of the high degree of predictability of what happens in real life and of what is portrayed on the stage. Our life scripts have a prescribed cast of characters, dialogues, acts, and scenes. People are seen as objects to be coerced, seduced, bribed, or recruited into necessary roles. Put another way, each of us has his own personal scripture of how to live life. It dictates where we are going and how we are going to get there. Most of us are not aware of how scriptlike and artificial our behavior is.*

The four basic components of transactional analysis make clear what otherwise makes no sense; we seem to have a compulsion to live a preprogrammed life. Structural analysis, transactional analysis, games, and scripts are interrelated aspects of our social programming. Scripts are more complex operations than games, but are based on the same ulterior dynamics. We seek friends and associates willing and able to enter our favorite transactions. These immediate satisfactions set the scene for our favorite games, which, if played successfully, fill the acts of the script. By this process we select ourselves in and out of each other's scripts. This is why we

---

* This subject is covered extensively in Eric Berne's posthumously published *What Do You Say After You Say Hello?*

relate to the people we do relate to and why others forever remain strangers to us.

The function of our life script is to maintain the life position of the Child ego state decided in infancy. It obviates the need to face reality straight on. We simply refer an event to the roadmap in our head and handle it per usual. We need not face the discomfort of checking out old tapes with reality and making the effort to upgrade our behavior. This explains why everyone seeks tenderness but no one seems able to give it, why people seem to never learn, and why intimacy is so rare, while games, rituals, and withdrawals prevail. The task at hand is to undertake living without make-believe, without evading the existential realities of necessity, limited choice, and absurdity.

Some scripts are positive and constructive. They call for the best from us and bring about practical and useful results. When others in the drama are well chosen to play their parts, a positive script can lead to great happiness. More common are the NOT OK scripts—designed to lead to winlessness, failure, or tragedy.

There are two kinds of "loser" scripts. In the first kind the individual indulges himself in wish-life or make-believe. He may dwell on the past, cling to the old ways, feel sorry for himself, blame others, and sound the lament "If only I had. . . ." He may spend his life wishing for Santa Claus and a magical rescue. He may conjure up a doomsday future of the bad things that may happen to him and to the world and live with dread expectation "What if. . . ?" Completely involved in imaginings of the past or future, the realities of the here-and-now pass meaningless and unexperienced.

Another common way to live out a NOT OK script is by striving to receive applause as a result of winning the approval of the majority or the powerful. When asked why they strive so mightily, these people reply: "I climb the mountain because it's there." The mountain is inside them. Such individuals achieve because by their efforts to gain approval, their internal NOT OK is temporarily assuaged by the external "YOU'RE OK." Congratulations from the powerful, rich, high in status, or elite are particularly gratifying because parental figures have always been the source of good things. Those delicious big strokes come from big folks.

Unfortunately both of these NOT OK scripts—the second less obviously than the first—are self-defeating. They do not address the real issue. Gaining a sense of lasting worth and happiness necessitates uncovering the NOT OK life position and substituting the OK reality. It is not easy to do this. It is to our credit that when able to choose, we will almost always be attracted to reality. The practical necessities of daily management reduce the attractiveness of dalliance with compulsive Parent and Child fantasy behavior. Management of people is a behavioral science. Hiring, evaluating, training, promoting, transferring, and firing bring about behavioral change and influence the individual's psychology. These can be done in a way to promote individual and organizational health or sickness.

To carry the drama forward, the scriptwriter has to attract others to play complementary manipulative roles. There are three script roles, as noted by Stephen Karpman*: persecutor, victim, rescuer. There are, of course, individuals to whom these roles are authentic. People in positions of power who, by unfair or unreasonable demands or rigorous exploitation, impose unnecessary burdens and hardships on those under their control are rightly called tyrants. The distress is genuine in those tricked, duped, or suffering because of the rapacity of another. He who frees another from confinement, violence, danger, or evil is a genuine savior. But many assume these roles in an unreal way. Their claims are not convincing in themselves but have ulterior purposes.

The illegitimate rescuer inflicts unwanted advice or assistance on another, gives inept or unhelpful help that creates more problems than it solves, fosters dependency, acts out of his own needs, unaware of the consequences for others, and uses rescuing to control. The manipulative persecutor plays the game "Gotcha," does not understand his own motivations, and derives pleasure from harassing others in a way that injures, grieves, or afflicts. The manipulative victim claims falsely that he has been badly used, for the benefits he can gain.

Usually played from the Child ego state, manipulative roles are designed to attract those in the environment who are

* "Script Drama Analysis," *Transactional Analysis Bulletin*, Vol. 7, No. 26 (1968), pp. 39–43.

suitable for the individual's games and script. Most everyone is able to play all three roles. If one plays the role as a "showoff" or wears it as a mask, this is manipulation. Usually it is not hard for the manager to distinguish the genuinely hurting person from the one who plays the role for its secondary benefits. Scripts have themes that can be used as titles:

Winning is the only thing that counts.
Committing suicide slowly with alcohol (work, drugs).
Failing at least once each day.
Bearing up under the tedium of things.
Creating trouble.
Not caring about you or anything.
Being top dog.

Some script themes bring happiness:

Seeing the best in any situation.
It takes so little to be happy.
Old friends are the best.
Being helpful.
Having a ball with people.
Surprised by joy.
Wondrous excitement of life.

Our individual scripts are decided by our Child ego state during our infant years before we had the equipment to form an accurate picture of ourselves, others, and life. Then our only guide was the reactions of others to us. We had no cause or ability to question these. We accepted judgments, communicated first by touch, feel, and sound, and later by gestures and deeds. These judgments we adopted into a feeling-decision about ourselves and our relationships with others. Still later, early experiences of our parents were reinforced by script messages. These attributions carry great force and tend to be convincing because they come from the source of all power and good. Parents have a godlike quality to children. What they say has compelling force. For example:

You're just like your father (mother, etc.).
You'll go far in this world.
What a lawyer (doctor, etc.) you'd make.

You'll never amount to anything.
You can charm the birds off the trees.
What a fine boy (girl) you are.
With that gift of gab, you can go anywhere.

We receive programming messages about many areas of life: family, work, self-identity, sex, education, religious values, physical health, ethnicity, and social roles. Some messages are fairly realistic about our talents and possibilities; others misdirect us to unrealistic or totally inappropriate goals:

This family has been farmers (miners, etc.) for five generations.
Smart people work with their brains.
You have all the marks of a good banker (salesperson, etc.).
Play around, but don't marry that kind.
College is a good meal ticket.
Wherever you go, Episcopalians are always upper class.
Ignore pain and it goes away.
We Irish (Jews, Italians, etc.) have always been known for good deeds (good fighters, brains, etc.).
The Lord made you female to have children.
Men don't cry in this family.

Some parents don't like their children. Mothering is not instinctive in the human female. It has to be learned, and some never do. A person who's never been cared for finds it difficult to care for others. For some, the process of conception, gestation, and separation may be fraught with anger, fear, pain, and a sense of helplessness. The infant makes difficult demands that foreshorten life's vistas for parents. While societal norms call for valuing and nurturing infants, some parents are indifferent to them or wish they didn't have them. Whatever parents verbalize, the infant experiences their true negative feelings: "You are a mistake," "How did I get myself into this," "Go away," "I hate you." Such scripts cast a negative spell over the child that compels him later in life to carry out the self-destruct injunction. Such injunctions Leonard Campos calls "witch messages."*

* "Transactional Analysis of Witch Messages," *Transactional Analysis Bulletin*, Vol. 9, No. 34 (1970), p. 51.

Here is a possible script analysis of an achievement-oriented manager:

Household drama: The child was raised to get his strokes from performing well. Concern for education in nursery school, followed by music lessons, Little League, Boy Scouts, religious organizations, and high school scholarship. "Getting ahead" was the goal. Caring was conditional on achievement. Parents were hard-working, moralistic, judgmental, and domineering.

Script messages: "In this family we're workers." "You will be rich some day like your great-grandfather." Family themes set early in life were later reduced to common aphorisms: "Cream always rises to the top." "Don't do a job if you don't do it well." "There are two kinds of people, winners and losers." Sometimes the messages were harsher: "Never give a sucker an even break," and "If you can't stand the heat, get out of the kitchen."

Script theme: Climbing mountains and getting things done.

Life position: I'M NOT OK—YOU'RE OK. When left alone, he experiences relatively high levels of discomfort. He seeks to be with people "of his own stripe" and immerses himself in work. Failure causes self-directed anger and depression. He does not always see his own mistakes as clearly as he sees others'. Games are goal-directed opportunities to further his own career.

Typical games: "Gotcha," "Harried," "See How Hard I'm Trying," "Ain't it Awful," and "Blemish." He selects role partners whom he can admire, look up to, follow, and receive strokes from. Or he seeks out those he can control, coerce, guide, and direct.

Time structuring: When not engaged in activities, he withdraws for rest and relaxation and to plan his next move. He considers pastimes a waste of time and avoids rituals whenever possible. A stranger to intimacy, he considers momentary human encounters as interesting sidelines to the important business of work.

Management style: He makes decisions and expects them to be carried out. Parent-Child is his favorite transaction. He assumes people are lazy, selfish, and untrustworthy. They need constant supervision. He is very concerned about production. He is self-righteously critical of what he deems to be incompetence and tends to hire from the outside to get fresh ideas and expertise. "Span of control" and industrial engineering interest him. He is in favor of training and other "frills" only if they sell more widgets.

Organizational dynamics: Communication is all downward. Organizational climate is tense and gamey. Parent is the most prominent behavior. Rumor index is high, feeding on suspicion. Teamwork is replaced by secrecy, and the rule is never tell anyone what you're doing, he may take credit for your work. Since authority is all on top, decision-making contributes nothing to motivation. Goals are overtly accepted and covertly resisted. Everyone plays CYA.

The feminist movement—both friends and foes call it a revolution—points to the systematic oppression of women and other minorities in our culture. Men and women have been scripted to see women as sex objects—passive, dependent, weak, vain, child- and kitchen-centered. Language has lent itself to cultural and social scripting. "Manhood" and "manly" are synonymous with fortitude, courage, and dignity. While "womanly" evokes images of vanity and lack of concern for time and serious matters.

Fairy tales are an important part of early scripting. They provide a way to objectify and cope with the fears of early childhood, under thinly veiled disguises. Fairy tales are one of the earliest kinds of programming we receive. They report roles, values, and transactions available between men and women. They are infant models learned on mother's lap.

Consider our most popular fairy tales: "Snow White," "Cinderella," "Rapunzel," , and "Sleeping Beauty." As feminine models, all are too good to be true. They are innocent, beautiful, passive, and victims. Their mothers or stepmothers, on the other hand, are malicious, greedy, avaricious, ruthless, and brutal. The mother in "Hansel and Gretel," you will remember, abandoned them, and another lady sought to cook them in her oven.

According to these archetypes, women cannot think, initiate action, confront, resist, care, or question. If they are not objects of malice, they are fit only for romantic adoration. Men, in contrast, are handsome princes, noble of purpose, powerful, and good. Princes are heroic, brave, stalwart in mission, dedicated to the good which they purposefully pursue. Early sexist scripting, as exposed in fairy tales, teaches that men are good whatever they do and that women, when powerful, are witches and, when good, passive and ingenuous.

The romantic tradition perpetuates our early societal programming. Women should be beautiful. This increases their attractiveness as sex objects and fuels multibillion-dollar cosmetics, advertising, and film industries. The rituals of beauty are handed down from mother to daughter and doubtless encompass the entire female body.

Western religious thought has also valued women mostly as passive, the keeper of the hearth and rearer of children. This inequality has been reflected in Western jurisprudence, where women, because of their supposed vulnerability, were given special consideration by the law and courts in matrimonial, civil, and criminal matters.

The Adam and Eve myth stands at the center of Christian thought about the relation of man and woman. Adam was told by God that if he ate from the Tree of Knowledge he would die. The serpent tells Eve that she and Adam will not die. Eve, beguiled by the serpent, eats of the tree and gives to Adam. The consequence, according to Holy Writ, is that Adam and Eve knew each other carnally. As punishment, Adam had to go to work and Eve had to bear children in pain. What was written to explain the beginning of things has been converted into scripting legends. On these negative notes have stood our understanding of work, sex, and family. Numerous commentators over the decades have pointed to Eve's cupidity, infidelity, and carnality as defining what it means to be female. The noble Adam was of course an innocent bystander.

Women have been considered chattel along with other items of tangible property throughout a history suspiciously defensive in its oft-proclaimed inherent superiority of male over female. It is time to demythologize society of its counter-productive view of one-half of the total human resource. Forces already in motion are challenging all stereotypes of women. They can no longer be demeaned by their special responsibilities in child rearing. By code, social sentiment, and morality they can no longer be relegated to menial work, denied promotion, and made to suffer the indignity of receiving less pay for the same work. Equality for women is no longer a fringe issue.

A knowledge of scripting can aid our understanding of how deeply these ideas are entrenched in the fabric of society and of what must be done to change them. Every manager faces the challenge of dealing competently with the sexist issues. Change is surely coming, and it can arrive at the cost of strife, pain, and confusion as it has so many times in the past, or it can come succored by reason, patience, and compassion. In dealing with our own shock as we face these difficult issues, it may help us to remember that those who seem to benefit by change suffer as much as those who seem to bear the cost.

The analysis of an individual's script is a long-term effort beyond the capabilities of the average personnel department. Nevertheless, since it is the souce of self-definition, an awareness of preprogramming gives necessary insight into the problem of resistance to change.

Because sexist scripting is part of the warp and woof of society and because concern for self-improvement is still a relatively low priority, most management and organizational change efforts take place on the social or team level. One doesn't expect change via the route of improving individual behavior. A more viable approach is to encourage a team, section, division, or whole company to decide what kind of organization the members want to be and to work with them to bring it about.

The task then is for members to move the organization from where they are to where they wish to be. In this task each individual is responsible both for managing his own growth and for improving the organization's style. Interdependency is the proven way. Those individuals who benefit from organizational dysfunction can be expected to resist change. A wide variety of "We've always done it this way" strategies can only be resisted if individuals are able to work cooperatively.

All of us considering our own resistance to change on the sexism issue have to consider the four basic elements of our own preprogramming.

□ We must be aware of the aphorisms, fairy tales, and myths we use on the subject of women, their role in business, family, and relationships with males. What are the implications of pornography and smutty stories? What script messages did we receive in these areas?

□ In business relationships with women, what ego states are operative? Are the primary transactions Parent-Child, Child-Child, and Child-Parent? How often do we see male-female transactions that are Adult-Adult?

□ How can Adult-Adult male-female transactions be encouraged? Are the transactions direct or ulterior? If they are ulterior, what male-female games are played in the office? Are "Cavalier" and "Rapo" played? What about "Blemish," "Poor Me," or "Wooden Leg"?

□ How do males and females use their time together at work? How much is activity and authentic encounter? How much is ritual, pastimes, and games? What life positions do males and females transact from? What is the index of authentic strokes given to all three ego states?

While some scripts are fairly realistic and helpful, others misdirect individuals onto self-destroying paths. By analyzing the various components—ego states, life position, transactions, games, strokes, and time usage—the well-trained manager becomes aware of his early childhood decisions that survive to affect everything he does. Line by line these can be surfaced and tested against present reality. Decisions can be made in real time, based on objective reality. He can stop being afraid, defeating himself, playing games, and losing. This is how scripts are changed.

Script analysis for the role of women would contain some of these elements:

Household drama: Being unladylike is the harshest criticism a young girl can get. "Go play with dolls and doll houses." "Don't play rough 'boy' sports." She is raised to anticipate the wants and needs of others, especially men, and to get strokes by stroking others first. Personal grooming and dressing properly are emphasized. She is early introduced to cosmetics as a way to please men. Because husbands and children are to be her career, her major transaction is Adaptive Child–Nurturing Parent. As a young woman she acts out one side of the AC-NP transaction, and as a wife and mother she acts out the other. Avoiding controversy and smoothing over antagonisms are her style.

Script message: It's unwomanly to be intellectual. If you want a man, play dumb. A woman's body is her most important asset. The Lord made you female to have children and to please your husband. "Isn't she cute?" "She'll make a wonderful mother some day."

Script theme: Always being nice.

Life position: I'M NOT OK—YOU'RE OK. She gets her strokes through the success of her husband and children. Her attempts to establish a position of personal competence will be viewed as being at the sacrifice of her children and husband.

Typical games: "Poor Me," "Wooden Leg," "Making Do," "I Was Only Trying to Help You," "Rapo."

Time structure: As part of her social role, she is taught to support social ritual and pastimes. Activities are related to children and house. If victimized by poor parenting, she may be gamey. Opportunities for authentic encounter are, except for a few fortunate women, almost nonexistent.

Management style: Working conditions and human relations are central for the female executive concerned with keeping people as comfortable as possible. "No problem is so big you can't overlook it." She believes that things will straighten themselves out if they are left alone. People work best when they are one big, happy family. She tries to avoid making performance appraisals, but when she must make them, they have a cheery, upbeat note. The approach of pouring oil on troubled waters tends to keep issues buried and may prevent the critical ones from surfacing. For her, soldiering is the name of the game.

Organizational dynamics: Even when people feel they can discuss company issues, they do so guardedly. Communication is mostly downward. Information that the boss wants to hear flows freely. Other data is restricted and filtered. Decisions are made topside by those who may be aware of employee opinions. Teamwork is minimal. After orders are issued, the female manager tries to put the best possible face on them while giving employees the opportunity to air their "beefs." Uncomfortable situations are avoided at all costs.

It was probably inevitable that the changing relationships between men and women would be characterized as the Women's Liberation Movement. The bad jokes and nervous laughter one hears cannot hide the underlying seriousness of these developments. The Human Liberation Movement would be more apt, since men are as much the beneficiaries as women.

What we are being liberated from are the age-old scriptings that cast human relationships into a cynical and rigid framework that maximized the cost of caring. In our society it is easy to give the highest commendations to those who as a profession pursue killing. We do not reward equally those who strive to promote human charity.

Because of its size and growing momentum, it may safely be called a movement, if we do not forget that it takes place inside of individuals, one at a time. And like all change, it is accompanied by a certain amount of pain. Women who leave the security of their roles as wives and mothers to face the difficulties of learning new roles in business are demanding our support. Equality of opportunity and pay has now become a goal of American business. If one is cynical about business motivation, one cannot challenge its essential reasonableness.

What are some of the things committed feminist managers have learned? Women now expect full equality of job opportunity and are not interested in confinement to secretarial work. Today we find women working effectively in areas where only recently we thought the work was too dirty, heavy, or hazardous. In addition to new educational opportunities new operational responsibilities must be made available. It is generally agreed there is no promotion a woman should be denied the opportunity to bid for simply because of her sex. The feminist manager will understand the necessity of providing support for those who are attempting new behavior. The use of power—so easy to so many men—has been scripted out of women. They are going to have to discover a new facet of themselves, just as men who have a scripted incapacity for caring must learn the skill of giving nurturing strokes. In liberation, both women and men are offered new possibilities that are certain to benefit organizational integration and productivity.

9

counseling

IT IS DIFFICULT for managers to give and receive help. On the one hand, being supportive may be considered patronizing and meddlesome as well as a negative commentary on another's ability—as evidenced by the remark, "When people are nice to me, I become suspicious of their motivations." On the other hand, organizational norms may brand one who asks for help as dependent and immature.

Many individuals operate out of the competitive rule "Never give the other guy the upper hand." This is another example of prescientific norms alienating people and corroding social integration. Instead of being a resource for caring, support, and problem-solving, people are problems to be avoided or occasions of embarrassment. Concern for another can safely be expressed only in the most ritualized and platitudinous way. With this inversion of human values, it is small wonder that companies function at all. The fact is that some—like W. T. Grant—don't and others manifest curious coping strategies.

The central purpose of counseling is to assist employees in liberating and strengthening their Adult ego state. With a strengthened Adult, employees come to recognize and overcome irrational and patterned behavior. One of the benefits for the organization is the increase in the rational horsepower of its members. After the individual has made the effort to identify his own Parent, Adult, and Child, to separate them and to strengthen their boundaries, he is able to put his Adult to work in behalf of fellow employees. He spends time counseling his people because be believes supporting others is part of his job. People represent a resource from which, if he invests wisely, he can anticipate significant benefits. He enjoys watching people grow and accept greater responsibility for themselves and their work.

Some professionals in the field argue that counseling is an impossible and thankless task in which there is insufficient return for the effort. The employee, they argue, has spent most of his life responding to the demands of others. All social institutions demand and reward obedience. An employee desires neither the stress involved in self-actualization nor the implied greater responsibility that would flow from it. His main interest, they argue, is to live comfortably, free of responsibility. The manager's task is to respect this and, with solicitude and skilled stroking, to help him survive as comfortably as possible within his position and station. To attempt to destabilize the employee's present condition in order to bring about growth will only beget resentment and appear as an unwarranted intrusion in his personal life.

While every person must be free to choose his own course and rate at which he can proceed, a responsible manager does not assume that an employee who exists only on the sustenance level and is not facing his life issues cannot achieve more. Company vitality is related to individual motivation, which is related to an individual's experience of growth and achievement and of feeling cared for. It is a matter of value orientation. If we treat people as inferior, irresponsible, and lazy, they tend to become so. If treated as responsible, independent, creative, and goal-achieving, they tend to act this way. Each employee should be offered the opportunity, and encouraged and challenged, to develop his full potential. The company reward system can be used imaginatively to encourage professional and personal growth, which will in turn encourage organizational innovation, vitality, and productivity.

HOW DOES THE PAST influence our present behavior? The brain is a high-fidelity video-tape recorder where everything which has been in our conscious awareness is taken down in detail and can, when the cortex is restimulated, be played back in the present as behavior. Stored there are details as well as feelings, interpretations, and behavioral adaptations. Although things are stored in serial order, they are indexed like a library. All experiences related to a given subject are found in one section. This makes possible judgment of similarities and differences.

When the cortex is restimulated through mechanical, chemical, or natural ways, we "relive" past experiences. It is more than memory or photographic reproduction. We actually experience again the emotion which was originally produced in us and are aware of the interpretations, whether true or false, that we gave to the earlier experience.

The following brief case study may be illuminating. Harry couldn't explain why everything Joe did made him angry. He first became aware of his behavior when the president of the company asked if there was "bad blood" between the two of them. Somehow everything Joe did seemed wrong and irritated Harry. Since Joe's behavior was not necessarily different from that of any other manager on the team, there was nothing in Harry's conscious thought to explain his feelings toward Joe.

When asked if Joe reminded him of anyone in his earlier life, Harry said he didn't think so. Later in the week Harry called his consultant and said he thought he had uncovered something. Harry's father had been in business with a man named Joe who had stolen his father's half of the business. As a consequence the family, which had been comfortable, fell on hard times. The death of Harry's father made it necessary for Harry to leave college to work to support the family. Since both Joes were from the same city, they shared some speech patterns and mannerisms.

When given the opportunity to let off steam on the issue of his father's failure and death, Harry's anger abated. He came to see his fellow manager as a unique individual.

This example demonstrates how our feelings influence the present long after the original cause has been forgotten. Events occurred in this order:

Harry was hurt, frustrated, and angry when his cheated father died and left him with the responsibility for the family. Certain things about Joe's behavior stimulated Harry to relive his original anger. Harry experienced feelings in the present which were first recorded 20 years ago, when he was 16. After discharge of the pent-up bad feelings, Harry's feelings related to his father were changed. Whereas earlier he was displaced into the past by the restimulated, spontaneous, involuntary feeling "I am there," now he consciously *remembers* the feeling that initially he relived. He still feels vague anger when thinking about his childhood, but it no longer controls him. Now in his Adult, Harry remembers the feeling—a conscious, voluntary thinking about a past event. By what I call "split attention" he can experience archaic feelings, with his own intelligence in firm control. Much of what we relive, we cannot remember.

Good feelings are evoked by the same process. All people have experienced great pleasure when restimulated by a line of music, a smell, or a fleeting glimpse. Sometimes it's so momentary, it goes unnoticed. It is easier to uncover good feelings than bad ones.

The memory record remains intact even after our ability to recall it has disappeared. Past feelings have the quality of seeming to be in the present because they force themselves on our attention. Through counseling, an individual is able to discover how his feelings are rooted in the past, and not in the here-and-now. When the feeling passes and the Adult surfaces, he recognizes the feeling as a vivid experience from the past.

Some General Considerations Relating to Counseling

The manager has to unlearn the negative material in his Parent which insists that counseling others is worthless, weak, or dangerous and can be undertaken by specialists only. Helping people to discharge bad feelings and to strengthen their intelligence is a fundamental healing process which can be undertaken by any individual who can discriminate ego state behavior and liberate his own Adult. Strength comes from practice.

With a little experience the typical manager finds himself able to assist others to regain some of the tremendous intellectual potential, gusto, and caring they were born with. The healing process is built into people and is as natural as breathing. It is irrational fears and counterproductive cultural norms that keep us from giving meaningful support to one another, but these are barriers which can be overcome. Understanding counseling theory and practice is the place to start.

The sales manager was warm and amiable and made friends easily. His native good sense and generosity helped him establish an enviable record. His promotion to regional sales manager was hailed by all. The company was sure they had a winner.

Two problems surfaced when he assumed his responsibilities as manager. First, as a salesman he had fought for his customers and left to the company the role of defending its own pricing policies. As manager, however, he had to resist his self-serving impulses and balance a host of complex factors. His Child ego state, which had served him well as a salesman, had to be balanced with a stronger Adult demanded by new responsibilities. Second, salespersons and customers alike brought problems to him when he became manager because he listened well.

He found himself highly inner conflicted. New responsibilities made demands on him that he hadn't met before. Some skills that had served him well as a salesman had become obsolete. In his new role he had to maintain a relatively impartial pricing policy and meet the expectations of those reporting to him. Meeting these expectations took increasing amounts of his time. Sometimes his easy friendship style made it difficult to hold the company line on prices.

To help him sort out the different elements of his own behavior, use his time better, and give him increased confidence as a counselor, the personnel director suggested that he attend a workshop to learn basic TA concepts. He learned to properly distinguish his ego states and to use the one most appropriate to the problem and found that he had matters under much better control. Only a year later, because of his strengthened Adult, he had a firm grip on pricing and had successfully worked through a number of counseling problems. Behavior training had strengthened his Adult and enabled him to maximize his native ability.

Since time is always a limiting factor, making an Adult contract has proved a useful part of counseling. The manager agrees to consult with an employee when the meeting is directed toward a specific change that the employee seeks to make. This necessitates that the client (employee) accept responsibility for the process and be clear about what it is he desires to accomplish.

The aim is to make the contract Adult-Adult, instead of Parent-Child, which is the agreement usually reached in this situation. Equipping the client to make an Adult-Adult contract is part of the counselor's task. The client must have at least minimal ability to identify his own discomfort and to distinguish between opinion, feeling, and rational behavior. The contract establishes the details of (1) the specific change the employee seeks to make (goal); (2) the time agenda and limits; (3) the use of the TA model, language, and concepts; and (4) the co-counseling relationship. Contract goals that employees have sought and obtained in reaching help include these:

Overcoming bad feelings toward another employee.
Ending dependence on alcohol.
Controlling anger.
Establishing a new relationship or improving an old one.
Overcoming immobilizing fear of a boss.
Accepting managerial responsibility.
Facing death.
Reducing the power of depression.
Ceasing to play the game "Gotcha."
Working in a more relaxed state.
Stopping nervous laughter.
Using the Adult more often.
Acting in more caring ways.

Typical contracts usually include three to six meetings, each lasting about an hour. Meetings may take place at lunch, after work hours, or during breaks. Early counseling sessions may reveal that the "presenting problem" is not the one blocking intelligence or causing discomfort. In that case it may be appropriate to renegotiate the contract. The ideal situation is thought to occur when an employee has multiple counselors to choose from among his own management team. Counseling is not the special business of personnel people. Almost any individual with a relatively strong and uncontaminated Adult can make an adequate counselor. Learning to make contracts, committing oneself to seeing them through, and moving to the next problem are skills appropriate to the manager.

Counseling is not an expert's prerogative but a basic element of daily human transactions. All counseling is really co-counseling between people working to understand themselves. All individuals sometimes need help and sometimes have strength to share with others. In each meeting both people may have opportunities to be counselor and client. When counseling is skillfully done, it is productive and rewarding. It requires conceptual clarity, hard work, and persistence to get through difficulties. With practice comes the skill to make any transaction an opportunity to give support, listen actively, encourage discharge, and support clear thinking.

Counseling is hard work. The counselor's task is to assist the counselee in mobilizing his own Adult to understand the past source and present consequences of his irrational behavior. The hard work on the counselor's part is to maintain his own Adult and not get hooked into the counselee's rackets and games.

In general, today's manager is optimistic about people. He sees employees as a resource for organizational growth and problem-solving rather than as potential obstacles to be overcome. He has developed the habit of treating individuals as responsible, independent, goal-achieving, and caring people. People working for this kind of manager and in this kind of company become what Douglas McGregor termed "Y-minded." They do not see people as inherently lazy, defeatist, or rebellious or destructive. Human beings act against their own best interests only because they have been warped by the emotional scar tissue of a lifetime of accumulated hurts.

The following explains how accumulated distress experiences contaminate and obstruct an individual's primary resource—his reason.* Intelligence differentiates human beings from all other living things. It is reason that enables them to make immediate and active responses to the environment. Their responses are not precoded in their genetic structure and delimited as to variety and number. The number of responses available to simpler species is fixed and can be increased only through the slow process of evolution. If the environment changes, their inability to adjust quickly becomes a threat to their survival.

The Adult ego state makes humans unique because they alone have the ability to create new and particular responses to developing situations that precisely match and successfully solve the problem. With their intelligence, they are able to create an endless supply of appropriate responses to continuous challenges from the environment. If we assume a world of infinite possibilities, reason is precisely the tool necessary to survive.

For all practical purposes, scientists consider the capacity of human intelligence to be limitless. We use only a small portion of our total brain area. Almost all have "genius" capabilities. Those who have more Adult available for their use are the benefactors of benign rearing practices and social circumstances. Those who behave in irrational and rigid ways demonstrate that something has gone wrong that impairs their native intelligence. Their rationality has been inhibited.

When the Adult ego state functions unimpaired, it receives a continuous flow of undistorted information from the environment. Incoming data is computed by comparing it with data already on file. New relationships are recorded and old relationships reinforced. Suitable options to the present situation are constructed and scaled as to assumed effectiveness. Probabilities are estimated for each alternative considered. This hand-tailoring of decisions as the basis for action is the unique function of intelligence. Each experience creates new information available for use in evaluation of later experiences. In addition to data from the environment, the Adult also con-

* In this discussion, my thinking was influenced by Mary Kremer-Hartrick, a Buffalo schoolteacher who introduced me to Harvey Jackins' ideas about re-evaluation counseling. It will lead us into an explanation of a counseling strategy.

siders feelings of the Child and patterns in the Parent as part of the decision-making process. In TA, intelligence means reasoning processes plus feelings, plus values. What goes wrong with this powerful mechanism? The answer is that we get hurt either emotionally or physically. We may suffer shame, ridicule, frustration, loneliness, boredom, loss, anger, or other pain. We may experience personal or group brutality, disaster, or cataclysm. We may endure illness, pain, paralysis, loss of limb, hospitalization, sedation, acute discomfort, or other affliction. While experiencing hurt, our Adult ceases functioning and our ability to see things as they are and to manufacture fresh and unique responses is lost or impaired.

Temporary loss of functional intelligence is only the beginning of the calamity. Information continues to reach the brain through the senses, even though thinking is stopped. This information, because it is not mediated by rationality, arrives disordered, out of proportion, and is stored in the brain just that way. Such skewed material, when replayed later, is not reality-based and makes no sense at all to the observer who does not know that the material was stored under stress.

Trauma material can also be recognized when it replays as uncontrolled emotional discharge, not evaluated and not understood. Still another clue to trauma material is that everything that went on during the painful episode will be reproduced in minute detail. The feelings of distress, inability to think, confusion, failure—all are recorded simultaneously. Such material, because it causes discomfort when replayed, is often buried and forgotten. Although out of sight, it is not gone completely. The effects of the buried distress can be seen in various symptoms, such as erratic behavior, character disor- ·ders, sickness, phobias. Two consequences flow from storing disordered distress material.

The first is that a particular area of intelligence is now short-circuited. The individual is no longer open in that area to receive undistorted inputs and to think wisely about them. He reenacts the painful experience whenever he is confronted with a similar new experience. Something similar in the present hooks the NOT OK recordings. They are switched on, and the archaic distress behavior recorded during the original trauma is replayed as if it were happening again.

Although the behavior may have been appropriate then, today it is inappropriate. When feelings, words, gestures, and attitudes show themselves to be out of touch with the here-and-now, we recognize distress material. Human irrationality and nonutilitarian behavior are a functional breakdown of the Adult ego state due to pain overload. This weakened link in the system remains "sensitive" unless, after the crisis has passed, repair facilities are used to strengthen the weakened circuit and restore it to normal functioning.

To illustrate, the head of a manufacturing division was a competent manager who wanted to be liked by his subordinates and went out of his way to be friendly. However, a bungle on the part of a subordinate would cause him to curse and threaten the unfortunate employee. People were always on guard around him, watching for the telltale signs of imminent trouble. They suspected that his friendliness was a disguise.

Recognizing that he had a problem, the manager made a counseling contract with the personnel officer to learn to understand and control his anger. During the counseling meetings, it came out that the manager had suffered physical punishment from his father when he received a poor report in school. Mistakes by others in the company triggered the old fear and angry behavior. Through counseling, he came to see the consequences of his behavior on others and its archaic source. He then became able to use his reason to tone down and eventually cease his attack behavior. Today when his Child is frightened by an employee mistake, instead of summoning the angry Parent, he uses his intelligence to problem-solve.

It should be noted that the new situation does not need to be stressful to hook the load of bad feelings and turn on old behavior. It need only have a few strong points of similarity.

The second consequence of storing disordered distress material is that restimulation of the distress material turns off the thinking machinery again. This results in the improper storage of more disordered material, and there is a spreading effect through the personality. The net result of this is a decaying effect, where the individual is predisposed to be more deeply upset by more things, for longer periods of time.

As distress experiences accumulate over time, there is a progressive lowering of capacity for uncluttered thinking. Problems in middle age are harder to handle than those in the teen years because they are inherently more complex and because there may be a progressive diminishing of functional intelligence. We assume that the average person functions at about 5 percent of his total intellectual potential. The rest is covered by Parent material and NOT OK Child feelings masquerading as Adult. Yet, no matter how obstructed, the great intellectual potential remains there in everyone.

In some individuals NOT OK tapes may have been reinforced so many times that they now play incessantly as a kind of gray background music to an individual's life. His intelligence remains open and appropriable only to the degree that it does not conflict with these filters through which life is viewed. There is a tendency to "select" only that material that agrees with the NOT OK mindset. Chronic patterns form a headlock on how managers view work, individuals, and problems. If the blockage is latent, it appears only intermittently as a problem. If individuals are aware of their life positions, they assume "It is the only way to be" or "Isn't everyone like this?" When chronic, these positions (e.g., fear, anxiety, boredom, grief) are demonstrated in all aspects of the person's life; they are revealed in posture, ritual behavior, games, clichéd speech, set emotional attitudes, and facial expression.

Such chronic behavior is the result of a lifetime accumulation of hurts that left scar tissue that impairs the functioning of the Adult. This explains why people with genius potential behave in nonproductive, unreal, and self-defeating ways. They can't activate their impaired Adult, shut off old NOT OK circuits, and get into present time. They must continually deal with the past.

There is a strong note of optimism here, however. The process can be reversed. Counseling is the restorative process whereby reason is unhooked from archaic NOT OK material, put in charge of the personality, and employed to problem-solve in present time. The damage and blockage can be undone. Lost intelligence can be restored. The goal of counseling is to stimulate the healing process and to energize an individual's built-in abilities to repair himself. When freed, abilities immediately go to work.

People were born to be healthy. They have to go out of their way to remain sick. Regrettably there are significant societal forces and norms that keep people apart and frustrate the natural healing process. They can be heard in such commonplaces as these:

Crying is weak.
Anger is inhuman.
Don't let on when they get to you.
It is unnatural for men (women) to care for each other.
Men are never afraid.
Cooperation is cheating.
All men are sinners.
Keep a stiff upper lip.
Always take care of old number one.
Trust no one.
Good fences make good neighbors.
Never get too familiar with neighbors.
Society is a jungle.
A man's home is his castle.

We are soaked in these attitudes. By preventing the easy ventilation of feeling when we are hurting, social norms disrupt natural healing forces and conspire to dam up our intelligence. Once installed in the Parent and selectively reinforced over the years in the Child, these counterproductive norms are hard to dislodge and change. Change demands clear thinking and confidence in oneself. It is precisely clear thinking and confidence that have been damaged by unresolved past distress.

When in distress at any age, the Natural Child in us will spontaneously and appropriately express his feelings. If he is allowed to do this without interference or distraction until the hurt is fully relieved, his intelligence will resurface and regain control without leaving scar tissue. Reflecting on the stress experience, he is in a position to add to his memory banks important new data that will be available for future reference.

Discharging feelings drains emotional pressure and frees the Adult to understand what happened. What might have been distorted and improperly stored now becomes ordinary information available to assist in future problem-solving. Equally important, the painful part of these recordings is "washed out"; it is not retained in the storehouse of scar tissue for future replay.

Ventilation takes a form appropriate to the hurt, such as laughing, crying, yawning, anger, perspiration from cold skin, trembling, wringing hands, screaming, gross physical movements. This is exactly what the hurt person needs to do. It is perfectly normal. After being hurt, we would all turn to another person and "let it out," if social norms did not intervene. Nothing bad happens to a person if he is allowed to cry or shake until he stops hurting.

Counseling is the process of allowing the "uptight" person to discharge pent-up feelings which may have been restimulated by contemporary events and are impeding the functioning of his rational faculties. Because these feelings were not dealt with during the original distress, they remain always ready to do damage to present functioning. The new-style manager understands that all transactions offer opportunities for counseling. In daily encounters employees can unpack their buried distress and restore their functioning intelligence.

In counseling, the manager maintains his Adult. He does not allow his Child to be hooked by the distressed counselee. He also resists coming on as Parent by avoiding comments such as:

Get a hold on yourself.
You mustn't let people see you this way.
Things will look better in the morning.
There's nothing wrong with you that a good, stiff drink wouldn't cure.
You can't let the wife and kids down.

All of this "information" is beside the point. Such judgmental comments interrupt the healing process, and each time this happens, the individual is left more lonely, uptight, and estranged from others and his own intelligence. The counselor aims to maintain his Adult as the reality base from which the client borrows while he reexperiences bad feelings. After discharge, the client's Adult will resurface and he can convert old failures into useful knowledge that strengthens him to face challenges of the future. Teamwork is essential because each time the client tries to reevaluate past painful events, he experiences the inability to think about them which characterized the original trauma.

We never cease trying to get the hurts out of our system. Daily, individuals seek encounters, reaching out to others, looking for an opportunity to tell their story. The coffee break and trips to the water cooler are opportunities for people to discharge some of their distress. Viewed from this perspective, all transactions take on a new clarity and poignancy. We are constantly attempting to establish a safe relationship in which we are able to unload distress material. This is what we always hoped for from our parents. Our most bitter disappointments are contained in such remarks as "He never listens to me"; "She doesn't care"; "He isn't interested."

If not prevented by absence of opportunity, a willing listener, and social norms, the Natural Child in each of us would keep himself free from incapacitating hurts by appropriate discharge via crying, trembling, laughter, yawning, or anger. Discharging is the way to heal the hurt and get over bad feelings. It is largely misunderstood that crying is not grieving, but, rather, the process of *getting over* grief. We do not stop feelings by shutting off the display. Suppressing our feelings only changes their mode of influence. The display or discharge is the way of getting over or releasing them. Tears are the way of getting over grief. Sobbing discharges feelings of loss, and if allowed to occur whenever stimulated, sobbing will eventually cause the bad feelings to cease. Trembling, with chattering teeth and cold sweat, removes fear.

Discharging takes place with "split attention." While the client is reexperiencing past hurts, the counselor helps him to maintain an awareness of the here-and-now. The counselee ventilates archaic pain and at the same time is aware of himself and the real world around him in the present. He divides his attention between the content of the reactive pattern and "real time." While experiencing rigid patterns, he strives to view them and himself objectively.

The counselor helps the client to maintain split attention. If he sees the client's Child taking over the personality, he will direct the client's attention to himself or to something else immediate in the room. By this strategy, the counselor seeks to reactivate the client's Adult and to momentarily relieve the reactive pattern.

After an initial Child-Child exchange to establish open communication and a friendly climate, the counselor fires up his Adult, makes a contract with his client, and with relaxed attention goes to work.

Important "do's" of counseling include:

Listen actively. In general, listening with our Adult is harder than it looks. Adult listening is revealed by rather active body movements and vocal responses. All of us have unraveled light tensions when befriended by a good listener.

Ask questions. The intent is not so much to receive information as to encourage and reassure the client and to guide and steer his attention. Asking questions is the most characteristic Adult behavior.

Encourage discharge of feelings. The central purpose of counseling is to stimulate the discharge of bad feelings. This is done by focusing the client's attention to where the discharge is likely to occur and by encouraging the continuation of discharge when it wanes or ceases.

Take a positive view of the client. Unconditional positive regard for others requires that the counselor avoid any appearance of discourtesy in manners, expressions, attitude, or voice tones.

Allow the client to retain control of material to be worked on and how far he wants to go. The counselor does not attack the client's defenses. Since ventilation is a natural human tendency, the presence of an accepting Adult is usually sufficient to stimulate discharge. If the client seems at a loss as to where to begin, give him an opportunity to discuss himself and he will soon get to a topic where he reveals his tensions. The counselor then seeks to maintain the client's attention on the subject until full discharge has taken place and he can discuss the hurting event as an ordinary memory.

There are several "don'ts" that all counselors identify early:

Don't let your Child get hooked by the client's affective needs. It is an error to assume that you are being helpful by joining in the client's feelings. In general, it is not helpful to relate similar problems you have had or know about.

Don't give opinions or make judgments about the client's feelings, behavior, attitudes, history. Coming on Parent tends

to hook NOT OK Adaptive Child responses. Parent-Child transactions will only exacerbate the situation and have to be undone later on.

Don't give advice or suggest answers. Such a position is far
too precarious, fosters dependency, and presents the client
with the opportunity to play the game "See What You Made
Me Do." The best answers are those the client discovers for
himself.

*As a general rule don't interrupt or interfere with dis-
charge.* However, some interventions may accelerate or deepen
discharge. The decision to intervene must be made carefully
and sensitively in terms of anticipated results

The goal of counseling is to assist the client in freeing his
intelligence from archaic Child dominance. By discharging
painful emotions and tensions and reassessing the experience,
the client strengthens his Adult. There are a number of
techniques that the counselor may employ to assist the client.
These range from the least difficult and taxing for the client, to
the more engrossing. The counselor moves up the scale of
techniques as the client is ready. If the client's Adult is
threatened, the counselor may retreat to a more comfortable
level.

Three of the possible levels are: (1) Talking in the here-
and-now; cathecting the Adult, especially when it seems
threatened by Child contamination. (2) Recalling recent experiences. When there is sufficient "free attention," the client
can report recent positive experiences and light upsets. (3)
Surfacing and discharging unmediated material from the past
not subject to easy recall. A discussion of these three levels
follows.

1. Hooking the client's Adult, in order to begin communication, build a contract, or reduce discharge pressure may take
strenuous effort if the client is deeply disturbed. A greeting
will usually suffice to bring attention to the counselor, the surroundings, and the contract. Assisting the client to avoid factors that restimulate old pain gives him time and opportunity
to invest energy in his Adult.

2. When enough of the client's attention is available, it
becomes possible for him to remember ordinary things from
the past, moving from the more to the less enjoyable. Dis-

charge will take place in the form of laughter, "rhetorical questions," and rapid talking with rising voice tones.

A question such as "Any upsets this week?" will lead the client to release tensions of recent vintage which would otherwise be potential additions to his storehouse of pain. The client is thus helped to discharge the little restimulations that have occurred recently and so to clear his Adult for working on more difficult issues.

The highest level of this step is remembering similar hurting experiences in the past. The client is requested to report his earliest available memory of the same kind as the recent restimulation, and then later to review similar experiences in chronological order up to the present. The process can be repeated until all stimulative material is drained off.

Subsequently, review of portions of the chain of similar events may be done silently. When the pressure is gone, some incidents will recede from the client's consciousness, and others will be spoken about with a new interpretation, sometimes opposite from the one that was held before. One benefit of scanning is an improved memory. Seemingly forgotten skills, knowledge, languages, books read, and courses taken which were once held at the conscious level by the client can be resurfaced and made usable again.

3. Since emotional control patterns are strong in the Parent, the client can be encouraged to use his Adult to silence Parent "No's" and to give himself permission "to feel a little." The fact that many control patterns are developed during painful experiences explains why soldiers find it impossible to discuss battlefield experiences. As long as the client has split attention, you can expect spontaneous discharge. If this is not forthcoming, look for a control pattern. Strategies for evading defenses should be used with caution. Ordinarily the client should not be encouraged to discharge if his resistance can be explained on rational grounds. Below are some common defense avoidance strategies:

□ Ask the client to behave in a manner other than one he customarily exhibits. For example, a composed client may be asked to fidget, a rapid talker to speak slowly, an angry client to demonstrate caring. The aim is to interrupt the rigid coping pattern and to encourage discharge.

▫ Ask the client to say good things about himself. Because of a lifetime of NOT OK feelings, people too easily denigrate themselves, often self-righteously, as in the service of humility. Believing the negative judgments of others is easy because everyone has been hurt by ridicule, attack, and put-downs. Related to this, the counselor assists the client to forthrightly seek strokes for his Parent, Adult, and Child.

▫ Ask the client to assume behavior poses of sadness, shame, caring, bravery, and so on. "Going through the motions" may hook suppressed feelings and thus stimulate discharge.

▫ Role-playing can prove helpful when the counselor assumes the role of one actor in the painful experience. However, the counselor should never let the fact that this is pretense be obscured, nor allow role-playing to obstruct the basic counselor activity of warm, interested, active listening.

▫ Personalization of nonrational objects sometimes helps the imaginative client get in touch with repressed feelings. If the client is tapping his foot, the counselor may ask him to query his foot on why it's nervous. The client is then encouraged to respond as if he were the foot, and to take both sides of the dialogue. If the client's fingers are clenched, he may talk to his fist. The same technique can be used for objects in a dream in order to clarify their meaning.

▫ When the client overidentifies tensions from the past with a contemporary person, such transference can be explained and eliminated by helping the client to discriminate past identities from present ones. Questions that elicit similarities and dissimilarities are useful, such as "Who does John (or Jane) remind you of?"

To succeed, a counselor must persist in ever-strengthening his counselee's Adult. It is to be expected that discomfort will cause the client to seek to escape full discharge. His Adult must be enlisted in the effort to see the matter through until full discharge allows the return of mature intelligence.

Developing competence to counsel from one's Adult is hard work. It demands conceptual clarity, development of understanding of meanings and relationships, and success that can lead to ownership at the intuitional and spontaneous level. If the counselor is thoughtful and perseveres, there will be little limit to what he can accomplish in helping people to live more intelligently.

By now, it is clear that the counselor's most serious difficulty is the blocking of his own Adult because of rigid patterns left in him as the residue of past hurts. It is important that the prospective counselor provide himself with competent counseling. His success as a client will be a primary factor in his long-range success as a counselor. We all need guidance and encouragement in overcoming inhibitory patterns and cultural conditioning against discharge.

Skill in functioning as a client—that is, in discharging and re-assessing our feelings—is of great importance. Below are some important considerations of being a good client:

Many restimulations are so fleeting that the Adult will have to be wary lest they surface, influence, and are gone without recognition. Their transient nature defies discovery. On the other hand, when major areas of occlusion are restimulated, the vigor of the Adult to withstand contamination will be tested. We discover that we have growing amounts of "free time" from predigested rigid patterns when we can respond to life in a way we feel is authentically ours. This is a most joyful realization.

Commitment to our own growth implies that we accept the responsibility to supply necessary energy and discipline required to maintain a consistent growth rate. It also implies maintenance of a certain independence from the counselor.

Work done on developing clear learning goals before the counseling session reduces the amount of time spent in contracting and increases time for counseling. Although contracting may be a valid part of the counseling session, it can also be used as an avoidance technique. Deliberate contract building allows both counselor and client to focus their energy on the same target. It also maximizes the possibility for the counseling to be successful.

Discharging on the unaware or unskilled can only cause confusion and "crossed" feelings. It should not be imposed on the unsuspecting. While ventilation can take place under informal as well as formal situations, clear Adult attempts should be made to test whether the situation is appropriate. The counseling session can be used as such a testing ground. Few situations are more discouraging than multiple individuals discharging at the same time without controls established by a present Adult.

The counselor deserves encouragement and courtesy. Everyone functions better when treated with consideration and appreciation. An ordinary individual can do great things when he is properly cared for and nurtured.

All promptings for development of overly familiar relationships should be resisted. Feelings of discovery, liberation, and joy will be associated with either the counselor or the client. If these are acted upon without thoughtful exploration of the assumptions and consequences, the consequences may prove disappointing for both parties. There are precious few times in life when it is useful to act only out of one's Child without recourse to the Adult. The essence of counseling is that feelings are exhibited under the watchful eye of the Adult.

Dramatic display should not be confused with ventilation. Use of socially unsanctioned words, cursing, and screaming is exhibitionism. Destructive and violent behavior acted out of the Parent is not necessarily good discharge or responsible counseling behavior. While yelling or screaming may on occasion be useful for stimulating discharge, it can be done out of the hearing of others. Likewise, violent actions when necessary can be accomplished by striking a pillow, jumping up and down on the floor, and by other means that do not involve damage to people or property.

Counseling on physical injuries should take place as soon after the accident as possible, before pain and tension are stored away beyond reach. Rather than seeking to avoid the reality of the trauma (auto accident, fall, broken limb, operation), we should "think into the pain." By going over the injury two or three times and letting the hurt hurt, healing will be accelerated, and the pain will go away without leaving an Adult-contaminating residue.

10

the here-and-now

IF YOU HAVE ONLY ONCE had the here-and-now experience, you are not likely to forget it. Achieving it is one of the goals of behavior training. However, there are formidable challenges to overcome on the way to its attainment. It is an experience of unity in which the senses are heightened and the individual experiences a feeling of autonomy and authenticity. This experience becomes the model the aware individual seeks to duplicate and maintain. Here is one trainer's report of such an experience.

I was conducting a training program for supervisors at Kennedy Airport. Everything in the room appeared to me with a special clarity and vigor. It was as if I was seeing things for the first time. I mean really seeing them. My senses were acute. I felt I was experiencing the real me. My thinking ability was much improved. I took in great quantities of material easily and it all seemed to make sense. I was aware that my consciousness was having a strong positive influence on the trainees. One woman commented that she had never heard me so direct and clear before. The experience lasted about 10 hours. I remember having similar experiences as a youth especially at summer camp. I have had similar experiences since. But that day at Kennedy was an all-time high which has greatly influenced what I'm trying to accomplish with my work.

This trainer's experience of "real time" left an indelible mark on him. Words cannot adequately convey the depth and power of the experience. Being in the here-and-now is an existential reality, as opposed to conceivability, ideality, and conceptuality. The analogue is the Natural Child before his parents and parental institutions have taught him how to live— that is, what to feel, what to believe, and how to think. He experiences life and himself directly, and he responds appropriately and authentically.

An important goal of all company management and organizational development efforts is that of assisting individuals to move toward authenticity and autonomy by eliminating all the socialization traps which stylize and patternize people. The goal is to restore or release the energy, insight, creativity, and intelligence that individuals were born with. We consider humans to be the capstone of the natural order. Yet, too often they appear only as appendages to some machine or tool for others' political schemes. Liberation is possible because all individuals start off with—and many remember—the authentic experience of infancy.

The autonomous state has fairly well defined parameters attested to in the literature of psychology and religion. It includes freedom from domination by arbitrary internalized Parent forces. When an individual is overcontrolled by his belief systems, his intelligence will be contaminated, and spontaneity in his Natural Child will be replaced by inhibition. His behavior may at critical moments be inappropriate, reflecting his parents' opinions rather than his unique response to the situation.

On the other hand, if the Parent is decommissioned and the Adult weakened, the individual must face the world from the position of the confused Child. He has a difficult time viewing situations realistically, and often experiences life as a roller coaster of delightful highs and uncomfortable lows. Under these conditions individuals have little choice as to how they are going to transact with the world. They can be described as "unconscious." This accounts in part for individuals' continually repeating their mistakes and seeming to be unable to learn from their errors. Their behavior arises from internal preprogramming rather than from an authentic response to the environment.

Games, a part of the programming, can be traced back through parents to grandparents, and perhaps further. "Those who cannot remember the past," said George Santayana, "are condemned to repeat it." Those who do not reflect on the source of their consciousness are doomed to remain fixated in their ego states. Unless they are interrupted, an individual's favorite games will become the heritage of his children and grandchildren.

The experience of authenticity and autonomy is known by the recovery of (1) potential for intimacy, (2) intuition, (3) heightened awareness, (4) spontaneity, and (5) sharpened intelligence.

Potential for intimacy. Intimacy or authentic encounter is the direct expression of meaningful feelings and ideas, without ulterior motives. The autonomous individual is able to present himself candidly to another individual, despite possible recriminations from his Parent, fears in his Child, and Adult caution which knows such exposure can be abused.

Thomas Paine said, "Heaven knows how to put a proper price on its blessings." It would be strange indeed if the rewards of intimacy could be gathered without risk. Yet the benefits of intimacy are such that individuals will always be drawn to try to experience it, even at the risk of anguish. Intimacy is the essential experience of the unsocialized Child living fully, with all its naiveté, in the here-and-now. Many recent studies and reports, including that of the Tasaday people, are revealing. Before they are socialized, most infants seem to respond in a loving and joyful way to positive stimuli. Affection is the essential element of intimacy.

Intuition. For the authentic person there is a marked increase in intuitive perception. Intuition is the coming to direct knowledge or certainty about life without induction or deduction. Intuition affirms that life is founded on reason, justice, and compassion. This conviction is not doubted by those who have achieved full consciousness. They simply proceed on it. It has been shown that intuitive perception evokes affection. It is part of poetry, music, and the arts and is sometimes called "inspiration."

Heightened awareness. A heightened sense of awareness so that seeing and hearing have a different quality is another capacity of authentic individuals. It is a recovery of the acuity of infant perception. In place of reason and belief systems is an experience of reality that is powerful and direct. Heightened awareness is what inspires great literature and music. The difficulty of representing it is the source of artistic frustration.

Jesus faced this dilemma when attempting to report his experience of the "Father." As reported in the Fourth Gospel, Jesus said, "I have many things to say to you, but you cannot hear them now." He emboldens His followers, affirming that in the future they will have experiences by which they will be able to understand what He had experienced. Indeed, He encourages, they will have even greater experiences.

Spontaneity. Authenticity and autonomy both imply spontaneity, where one's behavior flows from natural feeling or native tendency without either internal corruption or external restraint. The autonomous person is self-acting; he or she does things because of his or her own energy, without premeditation. Spontaneity means options and the freedom to choose from Parent feelings, Adult feelings, and Child feelings. It means not operating out of the socialized self molded by others. It is liberation from obsessive behavior.

The authentic person sees life through his own eyes, not through the eyes of others. He acts out of knowledge which he owns, which belongs to the self. He investigates life as it is presented to him and attempts to experience it fully. He is not easily discomfited. He does not try to be other than himself. He assumes his life will take a natural course. "Letting go" for him means allowing his life to follow the course it naturally turns to. Rather than being distracted by his own pull toward empty goals, he seeks a genuine relationship with people and natural life. By following his deepest heart, he escapes the inanities and irrelevancies of life. Where his hand turns easily, that's the direction he takes. As the saying goes, "It's easy to ride a horse in the direction it wants to go."

The authentic person has a reality view of his life and his limitations. He looks on the certitude of death with interest. Its inevitability gives all his experiences a certain poignancy. He knows what he feels and accepts his emotions and their contrariety with wonder. He recognizes the necessity of order and morality and strives to be as rationally effective as possible. In short he knows when it is, where it is, and how it is.

Sharpened intelligence. An individual's experience of authenticity is accompanied by improved performance of his rational equipment. He has the ability to accept great quantities of input without distortion. Relationships of things come to mind easily and memory is formidable. When the rational machinery is functioning at its maximum, it is easy, even fun, to work out complicated equations and pursue complex conceptual probability alternatives. Action-alternatives seem to be clearer, and decisions are made with greater conviction of their maximum reasonableness.

Before being able to experience authenticity and autonomy, the individual must obtain personal control of his behavior. This involves the discrimination and emancipation of intelligence from fixated ego states of the Child and Parent. Co-counseling friendships are fundamental to this. Related to emancipation of the Adult is the surrender of all the easy benefits of games and rackets.

After some personal control of behavior has been accomplished, a degree of social control of the environment must be achieved. The individual must free himself from archaic belief systems which do not correspond with reality. The special pleading involved in the individual's parental, social, and cultural background must be jettisoned. The fads and fashions of contemporary society must be seen for their vulgar and transient nature. Finally, the advantages flowing from one's immediate social circle must be abandoned. Then the individual is ready to explore game-free relationships and experience life authentically.

If you want to increase the amount of time you spend in the here-and-now, stop whatever you're doing and focus your attention on four realities.

□ Observe what you are feeling. Are there fears, confusions, etc., lying just beneath the surface, contaminating your Adult? Are important restimulations speeding by without your awareness? Is your body trying to tell you something—by taut muscles, sweaty limbs, or accelerated pulse rate? Get in touch with your emotional and physical feelings. Let your intelligence respond to them in whatever way seems appropriate to the here-and-now.

□ Take a fresh look at your life-space. Are you clearly focused on and aware of your surroundings? Can you relate them easily to yourself? What is your environment like, and what influence does it have on you? Is it comforting or discomforting? Are there things about you that cause you to do things in your head to make you stay out of touch with yourself and present time?

□ Have you looked into the mirror of your own behavior lately? Have you listened to your own tone of voice, word coloring, sentence structure, and attitude? Does it help you identify those circumstances when you are least able to maintain your Adult?

□ In place of real feelings, have you substituted projections, transferences, fantasies, and prejudices? Are your feelings clearly and directly related to the person with whom you are transacting? Give yourself permission to admit to what you feel. "Own up" to fears, shame, hurts. Don't let your Parent dissuade you from feeling reality, with which it is not in touch. Understand feelings are not in themselves good or bad. Permit yourself to acknowledge what you feel. Only by owning up can your Adult understand, allow discharge to take place, and replace archaic restimulations with authentic you-feelings in the here-and-now.

Authenticity means living in the here-and-now, not inside one's head and constantly dealing with surviving material from the past or fantasies about the future. Assume that you are observing four people seated around a table, confronted with a complex problem. As you observe the group, ask yourself which person is really in touch with the problem and open to receiving new insight.

George's main preoccupation is with following company procedures and practices. He considers the meeting an imposition. If people would only follow set-down procedures, these mistakes wouldn't keep happening, he argues. Oblivious of others in the room, he frets, "Let's get on with this so we can get back to work."

George's chief concern is how he will look to superiors—he likes to spend as little time as possible with subordinates, expecting them to handle their own problems. He is a conservative dresser, and he takes pains to put the best possible face on matters. His game is "Look How Hard I'm Trying." On a particularly bad day he will play "Blemish." Almost completely lacking in autonomy, his Adaptive Child behavior is most comfortable responding to real or imagined Parent control. In place of authenticity is inhibition and games of the knee-jerk variety. His ability to experience joy is greatly impaired. He may be a candidate for hypertension or a coronary.

Sarah is far out too but in another direction. She uses this opportunity to explain again why it wasn't really her fault, and to present explanations or excuses for her behavior. As a professional failure, she isn't aware of the secret pleasure she derives from someone else's ill fortune. It proves her suspicions of the ineptness of humanity and provides momentary relief from her feelings of NOT OK. Her favorite games are "See What You Made Me Do" and "I Was Only Trying to Help You."

Because all of her energy is used to deal with unresolved life issues from the past, Sarah is no more free to deal with the here-and-now than George is. She is almost completely oblivious of her surroundings. She selectively sees and hears those things which fit into her NOT OK scheme of things. She is constantly on the lookout for inadequacies and injustices. She will enjoy savoring them over cocktails at lunch. She too is not really there in the room, but in her mind remaking the world to fit her petulance.

Bob is the pro. He has made a study of management decision-making. He knows about force fields, bell curves, sociograms, and tolerance limits. To him management is a science. He runs his own department efficiently and skillfully and enjoys inviting the management team to use his most recent discovery. Secure in his knowledge, he is comfortable in his position which offers him multiple opportunities to ply his trade. He is proud of his accomplishments, which he wears like degrees displayed on the wall. He too is oblivious of his surroundings except as the arena to do his thing. He thinks he should write a book. He is very much aware of himself and his ability to use his knowledge to control. His Child and Parent derive satisfaction from his intelligence.

Paula is fully conscious and aware of the people and the dimensions of the problem. She is living in the here-and-now, and gives the impression of experiencing significant peace inside herself. She seems to savor life and enjoy her business relationships. Her thinking is not sterile, and does not travel only well-worn tracks, and her behavior and dress are not faddish. Her approach to problems is thoughtful and reflective. She always makes good sense. She has a positive effect on people, who enjoy being with her. Totally reality-based, she knows that now is when it is and here is where it is. She cannot be influenced by threat or coercion. She welcomes the benefits flowing from hard work. In short, she is an authentic individual with inner integrity.

As this illustration of managerial personalities suggests, the self-validating experience of authenticity is not affect, belief system, or intelligence, but a harmonious functioning of all three. When Parent material has all been updated and feelings in the Child are contemporary and appropriable, when the Adult is freed from contamination by both, the individual is fully functioning. The result of this is a new level of creative intelligence to bring to bear on the challenges of life. In authentic human beings lies the hope that technological society will not only survive but prevail, with dignity.

Self-relaxation

Self-relaxation, or "centering," is the process whereby individuals get into and maintain their contact with the here-and-now. Rapid changes of unprecedented scale, complexity, and newness are having a negative effect on the psychological and physical health of today's managers. "Nervous stomach," hypertension, anxiety, fatigue, confusion, aggression, and alienation are some of the disorders found in company leaders. The world is not likely to become less complex or more predictable. Centering or self-relaxation response is a skill managers can quickly learn to consciously reduce bodily tensions, clarify thinking, improve their view of reality, and release energy.

"Fight or flight" is an integrated set of bodily changes mediated by the central nervous system, which acts as a defense alarm system to mobilize the body against threat. Medical research shows that under the stress of daily life, a general excitation of bodily processes takes place: the heart rate speeds up, oxygen consumption and carbon dioxide elimination rise, the blood's lactate level increases (a well-known anxiety indicator), electrical resistance of the skin increases, the respiration rate rises, adrenalin enters the system, and there is increased blood flow to the muscles.

When the "emergency" response is turned on repeatedly, it tends to increase in duration and intensity. Doubtless in man's early history, this defense-alarm reaction had high survival value. In our day, it is counterproductive. Yet it continues to be aroused with all its deleterious visceral aspects when the individual feels threatened. There is good reason to believe that constant stimulation of the flight-or-fight response is largely responsible for the rise in the number of individuals with high blood pressure and is an important predisposing factor in heart attack and stroke. Unfortunately, since there is no socially acceptable way to discharge psychological arousal, it may become chronic.

Centering is a skill which seems to reverse the physiological responses of the arousal syndrome. It causes the system to tune down and become quiet. After only one "meditation," practitioners experience an improved sense of well-being and happiness, enhancement of their physical and mental capabilities, reduction of anxiety, greater efficiency, increased harmony with the surroundings, heightened creative intelligence, and a profound sense of peace.

Self-relaxation is an alert attention practice which allows the conscious mind (Adult) to experience increasingly more subtle states of thought. The practitioner functions at full mental capacity. The process does not involve concentration or control. Nor is it trance or autosuggestion. Research demonstrates that the changes of physiological relaxation during "centering" are more immediate and profound than after four hours of deep sleep.

Centering is an easy and natural skill by which managers make contact with the resources which lie deep within. A "higher" consciousness is achieved through a rested and relaxed body and a fully awake and relaxed mind. By achieving a state of least excitation, the individual hooks into a resource that many practitioners believe to be of unlimited potential. This state of raised consciousness is often referred to as the "true self" and sometimes the "transcendent self." Expanding one's mind or consciousness means tapping the unlimited resources of energy and creative intelligence that are essential parts of human nature. Quieting or tuning down the nervous system brings body and mind into synchronous harmony and clarifies thought. Done before an important meeting, it measurably enhances the possibility of success.

The following discussion contains instructions to elicit the deeply restful relaxation response.

A necessary first step is to identify our own "body talk." This is an important source of information about things within and without ourselves. Generally we tend to overlook body talk. There are two reasons for this. First, we have internalized Parent messages which prohibit listening to this vital communication—messages such as "Ignore pain and it will go away," "Don't pamper yourself," and "Once you start examining your own motives, it's endless." We have a strong aversion to looking inside ourselves. We think we should be *doing* things. This anti-selfishness bias demands self-denial, humility, sacrifice, and so forth. Self-awareness is too risky. One had better keep his chin up and keep moving. Don't look back. Remember what happened to Lot's wife.

Second, daily concerns of work, responsibilities of family, and the diversions of pleasure distract us. Subtler messages of the body and mind can only be heard when things are quiet and we pay attention. Even when we assume they make sense, internal messages are hard to describe.

Nevertheless, in "crossed" social situations at one time or another all of us have had an uncomfortable churning feeling in our stomachs and asked ourselves, "What's going on here?" or experienced vague feelings of unease or disquiet while listening to a speaker. In these cases, our bodies are trying to tell us something. The conscious manager recognizes these feelings as important pieces of information both about himself and about what's going on around him. He attempts to identify what he is experiencing and then to locate the source of the feeling. He trusts his body consciousness to be a delicate measuring device to "sense" what's going on in the social environment. Experience teaches him to identify those things which arise wholly within himself and those things he experiences in objective reality. He learns not to confuse restimulations of archaic feelings with here-and-now sensations.

Behavior identification is the first step to putting a finger on what is going on inside ourselves. By focusing our attention on the muscles and organs of our bodies, we tune into the communications system. Doing this systematically from the toe to the scalp is known as the "body sweep." The purpose is to discover and identify messages that we may have been overlooking.

Is your foot tapping? Does it itch?
Do you have leg twitches?
Are your legs crossed? Is one leg pumping?
Are you sitting with legs wide apart?
Are your buttocks clenched?
Are you aware of your heartbeat?
Is there discomfort in hip and pelvic region?
Are you erect or slumped?
Is your stomach acidic, churning, distended?
Are you breathing rapidly and short of breath?
Is there tightness across your chest?
Are your shoulders rounded or squared?
Can you feel blood pulsations in forehead or throat?
Are your palms sweaty?
Is your fist clenched?
Are your fingers tapping? Do they tend to migrate to the mouth area?
Is your forearm relaxed?
Are your rear teeth clenched?
Are your eyes tearing?
Do you have a nervous eye?
Do you have a facial tic?
Does your scalp crawl, and the hair on the back of your neck rise?
Do you experience warm or cold sweat?
Do you feel any unusual discomfort?

How would you assess your overall body feelings? Consciousness is not located in the head. It is distributed throughout the body. Tension in the body reveals unresolved matters in the mind. Anxiety or fear will be experienced in the pit of the stomach or reflected in taut shoulder muscles, clenched fist, and so on. By consciously relaxing these contracted muscles, to some degree we reduce mental tension.

Although it is a mentally alert technique, centering is usually done with the eyes closed to reduce bodily excitation by cutting off visual stimuli. It is not used to induce sleep but to clarify the mind and free up energy otherwise spent in maintaining bodily tensions. What is sought is a passive mental attitude where the intelligence is fully mobilized but not active. To repeat, there is no trance, no hypnotism, no autosuggestion, no loss of control.

The mind is like a computer whose natural state is to be at rest. Given a program to compute, it will do its work and return to the idle state, awaiting new input. To practice centering, seek a quiet place and sit in a comfortable position with spine erect. Reduce muscular activity to a minimum. Use the body sweep to calm all muscles and organs. Allow them to remain deeply relaxed throughout the centering process. With your eyes closed, first be aware of the sounds in the room. Shift your attention and observe yourself sitting. Then observe what's going on in your consciousness. When you are able to do this, you have achieved "split attention." You are aware of your environment, aware of yourself relaxing, and aware of what's going on in your mind.

As the body becomes quiet, you pay increasing attention to what goes on in your consciousness. Simply observe. Do not interrupt or interfere. Do not focus. Do not concentrate. Do not add or subtract; only observe. Three types of material will be observed. Material from the recent past will surface. You may be surprised at how much more you saw, heard, felt, and understood than you thought you had. You may observe things that you held out of the consciousness for a long time because its presence causes discomfort. If kept repressed, such material would block intelligence, drain off energy, and spoil your ability to see things as they are. If it surfaces, it will disappear. Finally, you may reexperience scenes from early childhood which now will appear in a new light.

All individuals are really children in grown-up bodies. If the scenes are pleasant, enjoy them. But do not interfere with or interrupt them. Only observe. After about 10 minutes, the entire system will be experienced as quieting down. Brainwave tracings at this point reveal the subject to be in the alpha state. It is here that he is most intelligent, alert, and intuitive.

It was in this state that Einstein first surmised the possible correlation between energy and mass.

Centering should continue for about 20 minutes. Open your eyes to check the time. Do not use an alarm. During the process do not worry that you may not be getting it. Sit quietly for a few moments after you finish, first with eyes closed, and then with them open. Two such periods each day seem to provide an adequate base to maintain the relaxation response. It should not be practiced less than two hours after any meal, nor last more than 20 minutes. Since the mind welcomes such a satisfying experience and the benefits are so immediate and real, little self-discipline is needed to establish a daily routine.

Profound relaxation can be enhanced by the use of a mental device. Two are commonly used. A meaningless sound when repeated quietly at varying pace over and over can assist in achieving and maintaining a passive mental attitude. Any sound or phrase meaningful or meaningless to the practitioner can be used. The idea is to listen and observe the sound but not initiate thought about it. If a thought wanders in, observe it. It will go away.

This device is usually a pleasant-sounding word combining long vowels and soft consonants. Examples would be "shalom," "roam," "won." The purpose of the repetition is to help you to cease all meaningful mental activity. The repetition seems to have a soothing, vibratory affect on the nervous system. With practice, the relaxation response will begin as soon as you turn to your mental device. Another helpful device is to observe your own breathing. As you exhale, say the word "roam" silently to yourself. Repeat the word in rhythm with every breath. Do not worry whether you are achieving a profound level of relaxation. It will occur at its own pace.

Because the benefits of centering are so important and real, it may seem that the process should be more complex than it is. People may not attempt the process because it seems too unimportant. Yet, real benefits can be obtained the very first time. The process opens the deeper resources of the individual. It releases what may well prove to be the unlimited resources of the human spirit.

11

questions managers commonly want answered

Q. *How can I deal with my boss? When he's angry, I become upset and confused. He doesn't listen and always acts certain.*

A. Others' anger may hook all the NOT OK you felt when you were a helpless child. Remember that your Adult is stronger than your Child. You can unhook from feelings of fear and failure. Remind yourself of the I'M OK life position. Use your Adult to make the process comment "I see you're angry." This will help mobilize your boss's Adult so you can both problem-solve.

Most managers realize the organization does not benefit when workers are angry, upset, and frightened. If their Parent behavior causes this, their own reason will motivate them to change. Some people act aggressively without feeling angry. They assume erroneously that this is good managerial behavior. Others aggress because they are afraid. Still others enjoy their tantrums. They enjoy replaying early Parent recordings.

Q. *How can I deal with a subordinate who acts defeated, demotivated, and withdrawn? He complains when I give*

him work and plays "If It Weren't for Him I Could,"
"Wooden Leg," and "Blemish."

A. Most people labor under the burden of NOT OK. Some cope less well than others. They avoid contact with people and problems and hope to survive on the favors of others, both large and small. Since they expect to be defeated, they manage to defeat themselves. Being with OK people is painful for them.

Use your nurturing Parent to seek out and support the OK in your subordinate. You might comment, for example, "You're very punctual and diligent, and you set a good example for others. Maybe now you could try harder to avoid misspellings and typos." The Adaptive Child responds willingly to nurturing from the Parent. This sets the stage to influence the subordinate's Adult. Step by step, the undone Child can become stronger by successfully tackling larger responsibilities, with the support of your benign Parent as well as the resources of your Adult.

Q. *How can I handle communication failure and the bad feelings that follow?*

A. Admit failure openly. If the accompanying bad feelings are heavy, go to a friend with a sound Adult who will care for and listen to you. A good listener mainly uses his Adult when supporting a hurt friend.

When the bad feelings subside, use your Adult to analyze the relationship breakdown. Create a transogram. Set up the crossed transaction you were victim of. Identify the behavior that crossed you or the other individual. Decide what behavior is more appropriate to the expectations the other individual has for you or vice versa. If possible, try the new behavior out before you reenter the broken relationship. Your new behavior should get the results you desire. When wisely used, negative results can prove more important than positive ones.

Q. *What should I do when I feel* NOT OK *and there is no clear reason for it?*

A. Remember that bad feelings on your Child tapes were recorded when you were very young. Since they were the foundation experiences of your life, they remain fundamental to your personality. Because the infant is totally dependent on the relative proximity and warmth of the parent, those early years may have recorded loneliness, frustration, fear, and anger along with warmth, joy, and happiness. Sometimes an "inner switch" is thrown and the old NOT OK Child tapes are turned on. Alternatively, old Parent tapes may turn on and begin "beating on" your helpless Child for the umpteenth time.

Your Adult is stronger than either your Child or your Parent, and by energizing it, you can unhook from bad feelings and the counterproductive behavior they may cause. Involving yourself in Adult activities with others is the certain way to turn off NOT OK tapes. It helps to do something that pleases your Child. While these old tapes cannot be erased, new pleasures and successes recorded by the Adult tend to reduce the level of discomfort and shorten its duration. This is what is meant by making the Adult the "executive" of the personality. It is hard work, but the way is clear and the rewards considerable.

Q. *How can I handle bad feelings caused by others' better offices, larger salaries, greater responsibilities, and more favorable life?*

A. From our earliest years, we have coped with NOT OK feelings by seeing things as the extension of ourselves. When people admire our possessions, they admire us. This is the basis of our competitive feelings and the oldest childhood game, "My red wagon is better than yours." Keeping up appearances is self-defeating because it doesn't get at the real problem of archaic NOT OK feelings. Curing symptoms usually is counterproductive. It takes away the pain and leaves the pathology. Coping gains achieved by status are short-lived and tend to put one on a treadmill.

The task in life is not to be a winner but to be authentic—to achieve an inner congruency and benignity where your insides and your environment work together for maximum joy, meaning, and productivity. Learn to accept your NOT OK feelings and to understand where they came from. This will lessen their ability to impair your functioning, and at the same time, strengthen your Adult. By not having to deal with the residual concerns of childhood, you free energy to wrestle with the problems of today. This is how frogs become princes.

Q. *How should I deal with those who aggress by refusing to meet legitimate expectations set for them?*

A. Some people express their anger by refusing to meet expectations set for them by the organization, team, or boss. Typically, they act Adult, put on the appearance of cooperation, and may even smile in a friendly way. However, experience teaches you that, without constant prodding, they can't be trusted to do the job fully. They interpret your actions and words in a negative way and, in extreme cases, may deliberately restrain production.

The passive-aggressive individual has an Adult impaired by bad feelings. Because he feels bad, he jumps to the erroneous conclusion that it's a bum world. He selectively sees those things in life which support his presumptions, and he behaves in ways that validate his negative views. Everything fits his cynical position. The approach must be to repair the damage caused by stroke deprivation. By helping the NOT OK person to feel better about himself, you make it possible for him to get a better view of reality. This is the first step in strengthening his Adult, which will lead ultimately to his owning up to and managing his own behavior. Although early strokes will be viewed suspiciously, when their authenticity is experienced, the trust necessary to open communication between you can be established.

Q. *What can I do when someone I like hurts me?*

A. It depends on how OK you feel or, alternatively, how badly you are hurt. If it's a good day for you and you feel strong, go to the person and tell him there are "crossed" feelings between you and you would like to get "straight" with him. If he agrees, describe the behavior (either your own or his), and report its impact on you in terms of feelings. Try not to explain, interpret, or judge his behavior. Simply report your feelings as a consequence of it. You will discover things will quickly get better between you.

Do not overlook hurts, slights, and breakdowns. They accumulate in a reservoir of discontent which may lead to self-defeating behavior and even sickness. If you experience great discomfort because of another's hurting behavior, it is good practice to withdraw and "get your head together" before you work the problem with him. You may have to "backtrack" on your feelings in an attempt to discover what hurt you when you were a child that causes you extra pain today. It is best to do this with a friend. As with finding a new friend or buying something, coping strategies may give temporary relief. Decide not to let broken relationships lie unmended; leave only the question of "when" open.

Q. *If I find all my energy goes into only one ego state, how can I change this? How can I activate an unused ego state?*

A. Observing their own behavior for the first time, some managers are surprised to discover that their behavior is dominated by only one ego state. Overinvesting energy in one ego state must seriously limit a manager's effectiveness. In general, when you want to energize an ego state, you should initiate its characteristic behavior. Since the insides and outsides of you tend to be in synchronization, when you initiate ego state behavior, the corresponding inner reality tends to appear.

Since "what you stroke is what you get," as people respond to your trial behavior, you receive reinforcement. By practice, modification, and repractice, your insides will become congruent with your outsides. As with learning how to play an instrument, by expanding your behavior capabilities, you will discover new levels of competence and opportunities and are likely to feel a qualitative difference in your life.

Q. *How can I upgrade my Parent tapes?*

A. When you act, feel, and think, without thinking, as you experienced your parents doing, you are in your Parent ego state. Even when we are not exhibiting this ego state, it influences our behavior as the "inner voice." The Parent in a great number of managers is too strong already. When they solve problems as they have always done in the past without awareness of new conditions in the environment, when they are closed to new ideas, when their behavior hurts others, when they oversolve problems—they have too much Parent, and they (perhaps with counseling) should seek to reduce it by strengthening their Adult. The law of the conservation of energy says that individuals have a fixed amount of energy to invest. In this case, what you invest in the Adult, you withdraw from the Parent.

All of us would benefit from clarifying the priorities and values we unthinkingly hold in our Parent by examining them in our Adult. Managerial values and organizational norms have clear and immediate consequences on organizational productivity. Any work done ahead of time on norms and values will prove profitable when "push comes to shove." Answering the following questions will help to clarify the content of your Parent:

1. Is it true?
2. What is the quality of the evidence adduced?
3. If it were true, what would the consequences be?
4. What were my parents like and what did they believe?
5. What frightened their Child?
6. Could they examine their own Parent, Adult, and Child?

Q. *How can I strengthen my Child ego state?*
A. Your Child includes feelings, interpretations, and adaptations of what you saw, heard, felt, and understood as an infant. If the environment during these years was friendly, you developed and appropriately use a whole range of feelings.

However, most of us adapted our feelings in order to please our primary parents. Because parents are coercive, we arrange our feelings to avoid pain and to achieve that all-necessary approval. We have replaced authenticity and spontaneity with a greatly diminished and stylized set of feelings. We have only to reflect on the "learned" pleasures a schoolchild receives from a good grade, or a homemaker from a dust-free table, to see our Adaptive Child at work. Because our feelings are unfamiliar and unused, getting them turned on again may at first be an uncomfortable process. However, if you persevere, you will enjoy a new sense of vitality and congruence. Below are some suggestions:

□ Allow your feelings to happen. Don't turn them off. Experience them—they are a natural and beneficial side of you. Use your split attention to observe as you allow yourself to "live a little." Give yourself the opportunity to experience uncomfortable feelings also. If you let them happen, they will disappear. If you repress them, they will appear in another form. Talking about them is almost as helpful as acting on them.

□ Describe your feelings. For example: "I feel afraid." "I feel like a little boy lost in the woods whom no one will try to come and rescue." "I feel confused." "I feel angry."

□ Find out where the hurt is—in your Parent, Adult, or Child. Your Parent hurts when someone offends what you believe to be true and holy. Your Child hurts when someone diminishes you. Your Adult hurts when reason is overthrown.

□ Figure out whether the trigger is inside or outside of you. Was the emotion you experienced touched off by someone in the environment or by your own internal dynamics? If the emotional response was larger than the situation warranted, you can conclude that something in you was hooked. Backtrack to see if you can identify the circumstance which set you off. When this is discovered, you are equipped to encounter or avoid those feelings in the future.

Q. *How can I strengthen my Adult?*

A. While your Adult is potentially your strongest ego state, most managers underutilize it. Do not seek to strengthen the Adult at the expense of the Parent or Child. All three should be available to you to use under appropriate circumstances. In other words, we strengthen our Adult in order to use our feelings and opinions more appropriately. Functioning like a computer, the Adult collects and organizes data, estimates probabilities located within the data in order to make decisions that lead to action. Most important, the Adult is the only ego state that functions in the here-and-now. Here are the steps to a strong Adult:

□ Learn the clues that identify ego states, and then discover how much time you spend in each. Do this by observing your own behavior and encouraging feedback from others.

□ On any issue your Parent will have opinions, your Child will have feelings, and your Adult will be more or less in touch with facts about the situation. Identify the content of each as you face a problem or issue.

□ This analysis may be difficult because many conflicting things are going on inside of you at once. Your Parent may be having its pushy say. Your Child may be overly excited. Your Adult may or may not have sufficient facts. Cool off your thinking by separating the content of each ego state. When the states are separated, you can dispassionately reexamine each to choose the course that is most appropriate for the outcomes you desire for yourself. This means not that the rational course is always the best, but that an Adult awareness of the content of your general ego states measurably increases the effectiveness of your decision. Thus, whatever ego state you decide to transact from, the Adult becomes the manager of your behavior.

Q. *How much time should I spend in either of the three ego states in one day?*

A. The P-A-C model makes clear that all three behaviors are necessary every day. The goal is to be able to employ the behavior that secures the consequences most desirable to you under the circumstances. Our major task is to react to stimuli originating from others. Managing our behavior means the ability to respond authentically and appropriately to the situations life presents us with. Moreover, the model points to the interdependency of the three personality states. Because of the law of conservation of energy, you can energize the Adult only at the expense of the Parent or the Child. Putting all our energy into Child behavior drains power from the Adult and the Parent. Disuse of any ego state will cause it to atrophy. The most effective managers have all three states appropriable to them and use them easily. Any day offers much opportunity to use all three.

Q. *What can I do to improve a relationship where the chemistry is bad?*

A. Assume everybody likes to have friends and wishes not to have enemies. Analyze both parties' behavior to identify operant ego states. Study the transogram to see who begins where and hooks what. Outline the crossed transactions that corrode the relationship and duplex transactions that signal games. Use your emancipated Adult to offer new behavior options to the relationship. After a short period of adjustment, you will see new relational opportunities emerge.

Q. *Why are some managers only Parent?*

A. It is surprising how much of business we handle from the Parent ego state, when often the Adult would prove more productive. Fortunate are those whose parents gave them advice to value others, remain open to new ideas, and accept the challenge of growth. Less fortunate are those whose parents taught them to value things available only to a select few, to be indifferent to others and to the past. By definition, problems are unresolved issues that cannot as yet be safely entrusted to our Parent bank. In dealing with such problems, increasing the pressure of Parent convictions only makes matters worse.

Much of our Parent is a collection of myths which attempt to explain the origin and meaning of things in the absence of verifiable ideas. Culture lag is the continued support of mythological solutions to problems when better insight and evidence are available, or when the old approach is demonstrably counterproductive. Referring problems to the Parent is failure of the Adult. Rapidly changing environmental conditions demand the use of the Adult, not the stagnation of the Parent.

Q. *I want to work in a relaxed, reasonable, and caring way. I know things turn out best for everyone under these conditions. However, sometimes I find myself shouting, using abusive language, and taking positions that in a calmer time I wouldn't really hold. Can I control this?*

A. Many people report having had the disturbing experience of finding themselves in a fight and wondering how they got there. The shift from Adult to Parent is so rapid that it often takes us unawares. When you catch yourself riding off on a white horse of indignation, activate your Adult, cool off your behavior, and ask yourself these questions:

—Is it really necessary for me to speak on this subject?

—Do I know anything anyone else doesn't know, and are they ready to listen to me?

—Am I contributing to the problem or to the solution?

You'll find yourself regaining perspective and getting back in touch with people around you. Remember, when someone makes a response in less than four seconds, he's probably parroting from his Parent tapes. Apply this test to yourself. Are you really in touch with the here-and-now? Do you see how your behavior may be contributing to communication difficulties? The process is not easy, but it's full of promise.

Q. *What's wrong with my relationship with my co-worker? I don't know why, but we just never seem to get along. I try, but somehow it doesn't seem to get better.*

A. One way to test a relationship is to examine the content of important transactions. Out of a multitude of possible transactions, five are primary. By examining the frequency and content of these, you can identify strengths and weaknesses in a given relationship. If an important relationship has gone sour, this analysis may tell you why and suggest possible ways to improve it. We assume in firm relationships that both sides will transact complementarily in all five primary modes at appropriate times. They are:

> PARENT–PARENT
> PARENT–CHILD
> ADULT–ADULT
> CHILD–CHILD
> CHILD–PARENT

First test the behavioral frequency of the primary transactions by answering questions like these.

1. Are the transactions in each set generally complementary or are they often crossed? What is the complementary/crossed ratio?

2. Are some transactions overused? Are others underused, and some missing altogether? What are the consequences of this?

3. Which transactions, if strengthened, would improve the relationship?
4. Assuming you are unable to bring about a behavior change, does the model suggest alternative coping strategies?
5. Does the individual understand his P-A-C?
6. How much Adult is available in both parties?

Then, consider the content of ego states of both parties.

PARENT–PARENT

1. Do both parties share values on important subjects such as money, family, sex, religion, children, etc?
2. Is either one or both of the parties opinionated and not open to new ideas?
3. Do they have an adequate capacity for outrage?
4. Are they able to take a stand with conviction?
5. Do they fight realistically?
6. Is each person ethical and moral?

PARENT–CHILD

1. Can both take responsible leadership when expected and desired?
2. Can they control appropriately in agreed-on areas?
3. Do they exhibit appropriate support (nurturing) behavior?
4. Does each have clear values about the relationship? Is he or she intelligent about expressing them?
5. Are they able to let loose of control when appropriate?
6. Are both open to new ideas, yet critical about easy acceptance?

ADULT–ADULT

1. Are both parties able to enter into matter-of-fact discussions of important issues?
2. Can they adequately balance the pros and cons on any issue?
3. Can they separate external opinions and archaic feelings from here-and-now behavior?
4. Can each use experts and professionals without dependence or counterdependence?

5. Do they use outside resources such as books, journals, libraries, etc.?
6. Is each easily provoked by Parenting from others or incited to impulsive action by another's Child?
7. Can they both accept the paradoxical and ambiguous nature of human relationships?
8. Are they able to function, unblocked, in real time?

CHILD–CHILD

1. Does each party have full range of feelings that he/she expresses appropriately, or is each a single-attitude individual?
2. Is either one comfortable with softer feelings?
3. Is either one impaired in his capacity for joy?
4. Are both aware of their feelings?
5. Can they use anger appropriately?
6. Can each accept weakness in himself and others?
7. Are they capable of enjoying artistic experiences?

CHILD–PARENT

1. Can each person be properly dependent?
2. Does each allow himself to be led and influenced by the leadership of others?
3. Is each one comfortable with the little boy or girl inside?
4. Do they both like children?
5. Do they find it hard to accept the negative judgment of others?

12

P-A-C
self-scoring scales

IT IS A RARE MANAGEMENT or organizational development effort today that does not include instrumentation. Instruments are particularly useful for reinforcing individual judgment and pointing up specific areas of individual improvement. Because P-A-C is systematic and the relationship between behavior and motivation is relatively clear, P-A-C lends itself to instrumented learning. One of the most powerful lessons learned from the use of behavioral training in industry is that individuals are very much more alike than they are different. Most of the differences between people are not critical. The point is that instruments are not used simply to discriminate between individuals, they also demonstrate the common core that binds us.

The values of using instruments are well known: They can help teach the theory of TA and clarify some of the dynamics involved. They help us to increase our self-understanding by giving us personal feedback. They identify areas of improvement for us to focus attention on as we build an agenda of behavior modification for ourselves. We can use such externally derived data to make a co-counseling contract with a counselor, a friend, or members of the work team for their support in our change program. Instruments allow us to compare the relative strength of our three ego states with those of other members of our own team or of managers across the country. Individual data compared with the data of others in the organization can create a collective measure of group process. If the boss's style is controlling Parent, and six subordinates characteristically react out of their Adaptive Child, some pretty safe conclusions can be drawn about the relative horsepower of the Adult in that organization. This can be a good first step in helping members diagnose their organization.

The possible disadvantages of instruments should be acknowledged so that they can be dealt with appropriately. Results should not be taken humorlessly. Managers should not overgeneralize the accuracy and stability of the instrument so that it loses its ability to stimulate growth. It is counterproductive to lock people into their results, and to begin expecting only a certain kind of behavior from them based on those results. Every effort must be made to ensure that individual managers do not get locked into roles because they are overdependent on instrument findings.

PARENT SCALE

Instructions

If you agree with a statement more than you disagree, mark it plus (+). If you disagree more than you agree, mark it minus (−). It is important that each item receive a plus or minus mark. There are no right or wrong answers.

(   ) 1. My country right or wrong, no matter what scholars say, is the only reasonable position for a patriot to take.

(   ) 2. To err is human, to forgive is divine.

(   ) 3. People look to me for direction more so than to others.

(   ) 4. I find myself getting angry with people who vacillate and are unable to make decisions.

(   ) 5. Strict discipline is the only way to run an army. When the going gets tough, it's discipline that separates the men from the boys.

(   ) 6. When in a tough situation, a wrong decision is better than none at all.

(   ) 7. Even though I always regret it afterward, I "fly off the handle" more than I desire to.

(   ) 8. At least one of my parents lost his temper with me more than I would have liked to happen.

(   ) 9. My parents were stricter than most. Their parents reared them the same way they reared me.

(   ) 10. I find myself criticizing and blaming others more than I would like.

(   ) 11. There are two kinds of people in the world—those who are part of the problem and those who are part of the solution.

(   ) 12. To be successful in business, you have to be tough-minded.

(   ) 13. When the boss criticizes me, I feel NOT OK and tend to withdraw into myself.

(   ) 14. More so than I would like, I find myself capable of putting other people down.

(   ) 15. When I feel defeated, I remind myself of how insignificant I am in the course of things.

(   ) 16. Being angry may not be the most professional way to act, but for me it brings results.

(   ) 17. One thing I can say about my parents, they had their own ideas about right and wrong.

(   ) 18. On a committee I find myself taking charge more often than I would like.

(   ) 19. Weak people make me angry.

( ) 20. If I am pushed into a corner, you can count on me to make a good account of myself.

( ) 21. If my parents had taken a firmer grip with me, I would have gone further in this world.

( ) 22. It is extremely important that leaders never lose control of the situation.

( ) 23. I like to be boss.

( ) 24. Frankly, I like to drive faster than most people.

( ) 25. My parents were very strong on believing in God and going to church on Sunday.

( ) 26. I tend to rely on the tried and true approaches to business and marriage.

( ) 27. In the long run, there's only one way: one man, one woman.

( ) 28. One thing is certain, politicians take care of "old number one" first.

( ) 29. Careful planning is the key to sound management.

( ) 30. Others may flit from flower to flower, but you'll find me on the conservative side of things.

( ) 31. I tend, more so than most, to make quick, automatic judgments.

( ) 32. My parents were right, it's a tough world and the sooner you learn that, the better.

( ) 33. My parents didn't care much for me, but I'm going to do better by my kids.

( ) 34. Families that pray together, stay together.

( ) 35. I think the United States should have the strongest army in the world. After all, that's what every country wants to have.

( ) 36. I seem to daydream more than other people.

( ) 37. More often than most, you will hear me say: "You should never . . ." "He must . . ." "It is important that. . . ."

( ) 38. You can't be too safe. Either America's the most powerful country in the world, or it's not.

( ) 39. I tend to become upset with managers who don't test and probe for new ways to solve problems.

( ) 40. Creative people are in short supply in business organizations today.

( ) 41. If you give the Communists a hand, they'll take your arm.

( ) 42. It seems to me that people get what they deserve in this world.

( ) 43. Members of my family do not display emotional behavior toward each other.

( ) 44. Parents show love for their children by maintaining firm and consistent standards of behavior.

(   ) 45. It's nonsense to say my personality was set before I was 6 years old.

(   ) 46. There are times when people must do things they don't like, because it's good for them.

(   ) 47. When profits are going downhill, you need a strong and tough-minded leader to turn the organization around.

(   ) 48. A problem we always have in organizations is that people don't have the courage of their convictions.

(   ) 49. One thing I know in the business world is that you have to be competitive to succeed.

(   ) 50. I was taught early in life that it doesn't pay to buck the system.

(   ) 51. I sometimes take too long making up my mind, but it's hard to be confident in days like these.

(   ) 52. Frankly speaking, some of the things preachers say are ridiculous.

(   ) 53. I get disgusted with managers who are submissive "yes men."

(   ) 54. There are times when I enjoy playing "Gotcha."

(   ) 55. I believe society would be better off if people lived by the Golden Rule.

(   ) 56. Censorship may be wrong, but there is too much violence shown on TV.

(   ) 57. I just feel more secure when I'm working for a boss who gives me clear instructions.

(   ) 58. I believe we would all be better off if we stopped drinking.

(   ) 59. A person won't respect you if you let him walk all over you.

(   ) 60. My parents taught me to love my country. I wish I could impress on others how important this is.

(   ) 61. I distrust people more than I'd like to.

(   ) 62. A remedy for the moral decay of society is for more people to go to church.

(   ) 63. I don't care where you are, honesty pays off.

(   ) 64. I enjoy having people come to me with their problems.

(   ) 65. We will always need prisons because you can't change people.

(   ) 66. One good leader is worth ten committees.

(   ) 67. It's commonplace that people who act bossy, deep down lack self-confidence.

(   ) 68. Frankly speaking, some things we do at work are ridiculous.

(   ) 69. I tend, more so than most, to want to get ahead.

(   ) 70. A tour in the Army is good for most people.

THE ADULT SCALE

Instructions

If you agree with a statement more than you disagree, mark it plus (+). If you disagree more than you agree, mark it minus (−). It is important that each item receive a plus or minus mark. There are no right or wrong answers.

(   ) 1. When approaching a problem, my first concern is to make sure I have all the necessary facts.

(   ) 2. When religious teaching conflicts with my reason, I tend to follow my own ideas.

(   ) 3. I don't believe individual and organizational goals are necessarily alien to each other.

(   ) 4. My parents taught me to be respectful of the ideas of others even when I disagreed.

(   ) 5. I often find myself in disagreement with others. I seem to think more independently than most people.

(   ) 6. Good questioning technique is fundamental to sound management.

(   ) 7. Damn it, uncooperative people make me mad.

(   ) 8. More so than many, I believe people's feelings and values are important.

(   ) 9. Experience teaches me that effective leadership seeks not to control people but to enable them to maximize their own strengths.

(   ) 10. I tend to be on the lookout for creative, as opposed to traditional, solutions to problems.

(   ) 11. Successful managers of tomorrow will be those people who can work productively in teams.

(   ) 12. My parents encouraged me to express my ideas without fear of ridicule.

(   ) 13. I find it interesting to test assumptions behind what people say.

(   ) 14. I seem to read more than most people I know.

(   ) 15. Even when angry, I work to appear calm.

(   ) 16. Sometimes I find myself unable to face problems.

(   ) 17. Compromise proves to be the best solution to most problems.

(   ) 18. My parents, unlike most, encouraged me to develop "critical judgment."

(   ) 19. More so than many, I believe people should use their feelings more frequently.

(   ) 20. I belong to more organizations than most people.

(   ) 21. Not infrequently, people turn to me for advice and counsel.

(   ) 22. I look out on the world with equanimity, as contrasted with anxiety, fear, and cynicism.

(   ) 23. I tend, more so than many, to remain calm when others exhibit aggressiveness or fear.

(   ) 24. I sometimes feel lonely and distant from people.

(   ) 25. My parents were open-minded people and able to accept the changes they saw about them.

(   ) 26. My parents tended to emphasize rationality over feeling.

(   ) 27. As a child, I enjoyed reading and finding things out for myself.

(   ) 28. My parents were long on duty to country. In some ways I agree, and in other ways I disagree.

(   ) 29. Sacrificing my ideas to go along with the boss is not my idea of management.

(   ) 30. I tend, more so than most, to be willing to try the innovative approach.

(   ) 31. My parents attended church regularly, but did not get angry when I made my own decisions about religion.

(   ) 32. I'm committed to my own growth. I welcome new courses, seminars, and workshops.

(   ) 33. I tend, more so than most, to think clearly about a problem and to plan a solution carefully before taking action.

(   ) 34. My parents were concerned that their children value reading and clear thinking.

(   ) 35. I am sometimes overwhelmed with feelings for my family.

(   ) 36. I tend, more so than most, to accept the uncommon and exceptional.

(   ) 37. It often proves difficult to think independently when you find yourself in disagreement with the majority.

(   ) 38. I believe the expression of feelings is important to individual and organizational health.

(   ) 39. Crying does not seem to me to be a sign of weakness.

(   ) 40. I seem to be able to be detached and alert when others become emotional.

(   ) 41. People would be better off if they accepted the necessity of discipline instead of always looking for the easy way.

(   ) 42. I seem to have more interests and hobbies than most people.

(   ) 43. Even when traveling in a new country, I seldom feel ill at ease or alienated from people.

(   ) 44. I have clear ideas about right and wrong, but hold my ideas open to the challenge of new ideas.

(   ) 45. At times I am capable of great joy and excitement.

(   ) 46. I remember that my parents almost never ridiculed or were sarcastic about my behavior, ideas, or desires.

(   ) 47. Sometimes I cry unabashedly.

(   ) 48. Some people don't like to compromise, but I find it provides the best basis for a sound solution.

(   ) 49. People seem to feel free to approach me with their problems.

(   ) 50. It is extremely important that honesty prevail in all matters.

(   ) 51. I enjoy attending school.

(   ) 52. Although compromising strategies, like bargaining and negotiation, are useful, I prefer seeking underlying causes and striving for resolution.

(   ) 53. More often than most, I seek a balanced judgment.

(   ) 54. I am aware that the ability to estimate future probabilities is fundamental to good decision-making.

(   ) 55. More so than most, I am on the lookout for new research, ideas, and directions.

(   ) 56. More so than most, I seem to be able to stay open to the ideas of those who disagree with me.

(   ) 57. Colleagues demonstrate freedom to challenge my ideas.

(   ) 58. Since negative results can prove more important than positive ones, I seek the underlying causes of a failure.

(   ) 59. I have learned to be open and comfortable with my body, sex, and intimacy.

(   ) 60. I seem to face the world in a more relaxed and confident manner than most.

THE CHILD SCALE

Instructions

If you agree with a statement more than disagree, mark it plus (+). If you disagree, mark it (−). It is important that each item receive a plus or minus mark. There are no right or wrong answers.

(   ) 1. I sometimes want to be alone with no one near me.

(   ) 2. I dislike being loved, but it happens frequently.

(   ) 3. In my work team, we share feelings of mutual trust arising from shared victory and defeat.

(   ) 4. My parents were warm and friendly people.

(   ) 5. It seems to me that I have more friends than most people I know.

(   ) 6. I have trouble staying on a diet, or stopping smoking, etc.

(   ) 7. I believe feelings are far more important than most people realize.

(   ) 8. I use laughter to get me through a tense situation.

(   ) 9. When I am in trouble, I tend to withdraw.

(   ) 10. I am susceptible to impulsive buying.

(   ) 11. The "noise" level in our house is usually higher than I would like it to be.

(   ) 12. I like to use current slang terms like "out of sight," and "freaking," and "a together person."

(   ) 13. Although others may not feel this way, I believe feelings are the basis of most of our life decisions.

(   ) 14. My parents used to tease and embarrass me about my friends.

(   ) 15. I frequently feel sorry for myself.

(   ) 16. I like driving fast.

(   ) 17. "I didn't make the rules, I just try to follow them," I have heard myself say.

(   ) 18. I am a better follower than leader.

(   ) 19. I get upset when I become angry and quarrelsome.

(   ) 20. When other people feel good, I feel good.

(   ) 21. More so than most, I tend to compare price and performance before purchasing an automobile.

(   ) 22. There are times when I catch myself talking too loudly or rapidly.

(   ) 23. I am more self-conscious than most people.

(   ) 24. I am uncomfortable in unstructured situations and try to avoid them.

( ) 25. I seldom tell jokes successfully.

( ) 26. More so than most, I tend to feel sorry for myself.

( ) 27. People often say I use jargon.

( ) 28. I always seem to have more bills than money to pay them.

( ) 29. I am very meticulous about the clothes I wear and tend to dress conservatively.

( ) 30. Sometimes I feel blue for days.

( ) 31. Suicide is always wrong.

( ) 32. I seem to fail more often than I would like.

( ) 33. My parents, more than most others, seemed to be afraid of living.

( ) 34. More so than most, there are times when I feel like running and skipping.

( ) 35. It's love that makes the world go round.

( ) 36. I don't get my own way as often as I would like.

( ) 37. I much prefer to support the leader than to be the leader myself.

( ) 38. There never was such a thing as a justifiable war.

( ) 39. There are some things I just can't resist doing.

( ) 40. I wait all year long for my vacation.

( ) 41. My parents never seemed to get it together.

( ) 42. I have difficulty balancing my checkbook.

( ) 43. I'm the sort of person who has trouble pushing away from the table.

( ) 44. I like to go to parties. They turn me on.

( ) 45. For no good reason, many times I feel NOT OK.

( ) 46. Racial prejudice is useful because it prevents intermarriage.

( ) 47. It just seems that, compared to other people, I too often get the worst end of the deal.

( ) 48. I tend to trust people more than the situation warrants.

( ) 49. I often feel . . . "it can't happen to me."

( ) 50. My feelings influence my behavior more than I would like.

( ) 51. I am more concerned about the approval of others than I would like to be.

( ) 52. I find myself getting into situations and wondering "How did I ever get myself into this?"

( ) 53. Animals are a great source of pleasure to me.

( ) 54. I want my own way when I want it.

( ) 55. When others in the room become angry, I get very upset.

( ) 56. My parents may have made me more fearful of the world than other people seem to be.

(   ) 57. When on vacation, I feel like I never want to go home.

(   ) 58. Most people seem to take life more seriously than I do.

(   ) 59. Honestly, there are some things I can't resist doing, although I have doubts that I should do them.

(   ) 60. More so than others, I seem to be affected by my feelings.

SCORING THE P-A-C SCALES

In each scale the answers indicative of the particular ego state are, for the purposes of scoring, called "correct" answers. The point count (explained below) for the total number of correct answers for each scale is the raw score. If an item is unanswered, it is incorrect. The raw score is then compared with a normal population of people who have already taken the measure (n = 200) to come up with a percentile score (see tables below). A Parent Scale percentile score of 30 means you scored higher on this scale than would 30 percent of a normal population and, conversely, lower than would 70 percent of a normal population.

For the Parent Scale the correct answer for every item is (+) except for items 13, 15, 21, 24, 36, 51, and 64, for which the correct answer is minus (−). Score each (−) in the latter category one-half point, and each (+) in the first category one point. Then compute your raw score. To convert the raw score to the normalized percentile score, use the table below.

Parent Table

Percentile Score	Raw Score
10	17
20	19
30	22
40	25
50	28
60	33
70	35
80	42
90	54

Highest possible
raw score: 66.5

For the Adult Scale the correct answer for every item is plus (+) except for items 7, 16, 24, 35, 41, and 50, for which the correct answer is minus (−). Score each (−) in the latter category one-half point, and each (+) in the first category one point. Then compute your raw score. To convert the raw score to the normalized percentile score, use the table at the top of the following page.

For the Child Scale the correct answer for every item is plus (+) except for items 21, 29. 31, 38, and 47, for which the correct answer is

Adult Table

Percentile Score	Raw Score
10	24
20	28
30	30
40	33
50	36
60	39
70	42
80	44
90	51

Highest possible
raw score: 57

minus (−). Score each (−) in the latter category one-half point, and each (+) in the first category one point. Then compute your raw score. To convert the raw score to the normalized percentile score, use the table below.

Child Table

Percentile Score	Raw Score
10	18
20	22
30	24
40	26
50	27
60	29
70	33
80	36
90	39

Highest possible
raw score: 57.5

INTERPRETATION OF RESULTS

1. The highest percentile score indicates the ego state you used most or are most comfortable with. If the highest score is 20 or more percentile points higher than the score nearest to it, this suggests dominance of that ego state.

2. If fewer than 20 percentile points separate two scores (or possibly all three), that suggests there may be frequent switching back and forth between the two (or three) states.

3. As a result of training in P-A-C theory, most people conclude that it is desirable for the Adult ego state to be dominant, accompanied by a possible reduction of the Parent ego state and an increase in the Child ego state.

4. Pre- and post-training measurements during a P-A-C workshop show the greatest increase in percentile scores to occur in the Adult, with a smaller decrease in the Parent and a still smaller increase in the Child.

5. Although sufficient data has not yet been collected, it is anticipated that role differences will be reflected in P-A-C profile scores.

BEHAVIOR PROFILES

Based on observation, research, and data already collected, six basic behavioral profiles can be described:

1. LOW PARENT–HIGH ADULT–HIGH CHILD. This may be the most productive combination, where the charm of the OK Child adds warmth, intuition, and creativity to the power of the Adult. If Punishing Parent behavior is minimal and values are held in the Adult, rationality is emancipated.

2. HIGH PARENT–HIGH ADULT–LOW CHILD. Able to switch easily between Parent and Adult, this manager is often a high achiever. His rationality is ruled by the demands of his Parent. Education and experience are essential ingredients to his success. Key question: Can he distinguish between his opinion and the facts?

3. LOW PARENT–HIGH ADULT–LOW CHILD. Infrequently seen, this individual is object- and fact-oriented. His behavior may be repetitious and boring and his relationships sterile and unfeeling. He has difficulty working with others.

4. HIGH PARENT–LOW ADULT–HIGH CHILD. Difficult to work with, this person is hard-working, moralistic, judgmental, and authoritarian one moment, and the next moment he wants to be liked, applauded, and taken care of. Working with this person is difficult because of this love-hate behavior.

5. LOW PARENT–LOW ADULT–HIGH CHILD. A Child-dominant person may be enormously appealing. He prospers

in sales and in organizations where personal charm and intuition are useful. Often he is not a good manager since decisions are made in the Child and are distorted by fantasy. For him the key question is: Who are my friends?

6. HIGH PARENT–LOW ADULT–LOW CHILD. Unfortunately, this profile is frequently seen in industrial organizations where "we've always done it this way" thinking prevails. This manager, by treating subordinates as children, fosters dependency. This domineering manager believes that "people don't want responsibility" and that "they only work to earn enough money to buy a new fishing rod." Suitable for the industrial age, this profile is hopelessly outmoded for the day of technology and rapidly evolving problems.

To create a visual profile, draw a line representing your Parent percentile score across the P column. Draw a line representing your Adult percentile score across the A column, and a line representing your Child percentile score across the C column. Crosshatch all columns below your mark.

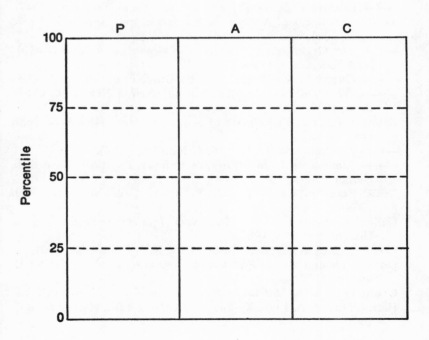

bibliography

Bennis, Warren G. *Changing Organizations*. New York, McGraw-Hill, 1966.

Berne, Eric. *A Layman's Guide to Psychoanalysis*. New York, Grove Press, 1947.

——. *Principles of Group Treatment*. New York, Grove Press, 1947.

——. *Transactional Analysis in Psychotherapy*. New York, Grove Press, 1961.

——. *The Structure and Dynamics of Organizations and Groups*. New York, Grove Press, 1963.

——. *Games People Play*. New York, Grove Press, 1964.

——. *What Do You Say After You Say Hello?* New York, Grove Press, 1970.

Drucker, Peter F. *The Future of Industrial Man*. New York, John Day, 1942.

——. *The New Society*. New York, John Day, 1946.

——. *Management: Tasks, Responsibilities, Practices*. New York, Harper & Row, 1973.

Ernst, Franklin. *Who's Listening?* Vallejo, Calif., Address O'Set, 1968.

Galbraith, John Kenneth. *The New Industrial State*. Boston, Houghton Mifflin, 1967.

Goffman, Erving. *Asylums*. Garden City, N.Y., Doubleday, 1961.

Gordon, Thomas. *Parent Effectiveness Training*. New York, Peter H. Wyden, 1970.

Gould, Roland. *The Matsushita Phenomenon*. Tokyo, Diamond, 1970.

Harris, Thomas A. *I'm OK—You're OK*. New York, Harper & Row, 1961.

Herzberg, Frederick. *Work and the Nature of Man*. Cleveland, World, 1966.

———. "The Wise Old Turk," *Harvard Business Review*, March-April, 1974.

Homans, G. C. *The Human Group*. New York, Harcourt Brace, 1951.

———. *Social Behavior: Its Elementary Forms*. New York, Harcourt, Brace & World, 1961.

James, Muriel, and Dorothy Jongeward. *Born to Win*. Reading, Mass., Addison-Wesley, 1971.

Janis, Irving L. *Victims of Groupthink*. Boston, Houghton Mifflin, 1972.

Katz, Daniel, and Robert L. Kahn. *The Social Psychology of Organizations*. New York, Wiley, 1966.

Lair, Jess. *I Ain't Much Baby—But I'm All I Got*. Garden City, N.Y., Doubleday, 1961.

Likert, Rensis. *The Human Organization*. New York, McGraw-Hill, 1967.

Lincoln, James F. *Incentive Management*. Cleveland, Lincoln Electric, 1951.

Lodge, George Cabot. "Business and the Changing Society," *Harvard Business Review*, March-April, 1974.

Maslow, A. H. *Motivation and Personality*. New York, Harper & Row, 1954.

McGregor, Douglas. *The Human Side of Enterprise*. New York, McGraw-Hill, 1960.

Meininger, Jut. *Success Through Transactional Analysis*. New York, Grosset & Dunlap, 1973.

Merton, Robert K. *Social Theory and Social Structure*. Glencoe, Ill., Free Press, 1963.

Milgram, Stanley. *Obedience to Authority*. New York, Harper & Row, 1969.

Missildine, Hugh. *Your Inner Child of the Past*. New York, Simon & Schuster, 1963.

Parsons, Talcott, and Edward Shills. *Toward a General Theory of Action*. New York, Harper & Row, 1962.

———, and Neil Smelser. *Economy and Society*. Glencoe, Ill., Free Press, 1956.

Skinner, B. F. *Walden Two*. New York, Macmillan, 1948.

———. *Beyond Freedom & Dignity*. New York, Bantam/Vintage Books, 1972.

Steiner, Claude. *Games Alcoholics Play: The Analysis of Life Scripts*. New York, Grove Press, 1971.

———. *Scripts People Live*. New York, Grove Press, 1974.

index